JOURNEY

A 9-Session Series on CHARACTER TRANSFORMATION

MAX MILLS

LU
Press

JOURNEY

By Max Mills

ISBN: 978-0-9819357-0-6   Paperback—LEADER'S GUIDE

ISBN: 978-0-9819357-1-3   Paperback—STUDENT'S WORKBOOK

Published by:

LIBERTY
U N I V E R S I T Y.
Press

Liberty University Press
1971 University Blvd.
Lynchburg, VA 24502
434-592-2000
www.LibertyUniversityPress.com
Editor@LibertyUniversityPress.com

Contact the Author:
Max Mills
mgmills@liberty.edu
434-841-3582

Cover & Interior Design by:
Heather Kirk
www.BrandedForSuccess.com

Our journey through life is uncertain. When someone, who has been this way before, shares truth about what is down the road, our future path becomes more understandable.

Unknown

CONTENTS

INTRODUCTION

W elcome to the *JOURNEY* series. This series is designed to be used in a study group with workbooks and a group leader. The additional notes in the margin of the leader's manual will help facilitate discussion with additional information, illustrations, and questions.

In every stage of life people are in search of truth. We are wanting to know what life is about and how to get a handle on it. Too many of us missed some of the basic facts along the way, that we must have, if we are to be successful in making decisions, growing in maturity, and having a rich impact on the lives of family and friends. This material is designed to offer help in finding knowledge, understanding, and wisdom from the Bible, which can be used to enlighten us on important issues of life. The information and illustrations will help believers and seekers to discover truth from the Bible and deepen our understanding of what God has done for us and how that enables us to handle life here and now.

Although each one of us is at a different stage of our life's journey, and everyone has personal questions and opinions, it remains true that the Word of God is the *truth* that provides direction along the way. As this truth is talked through and lived out in your study group, an understanding of our journey becomes clear, and the character of the only true and living God becomes more evident. People have a built in need to communicate with other people.

> **Nothing destroys like isolation.** *To overcome their isolation, American Prisoners of war during the Vietnam War communicated with one another and sustained one another by tapping messages through the prison walls. The "Hanoi Hilton," says ex-Air Force pilot Ron Bliss, "sounded like a den of runaway*

When we were just getting started in our walk with Christ, we felt that within the Christian community we didn't have much of an opportunity to be a "part of the act." And not knowing a great deal about Scripture, we figured that there was very little demand for our "song and dance."

The more mature believers seemed to have their "act all together," so assuming that there was no part for an amateur at the moment, we just "waited in the wings for our cue."*

* This introduction was adapted from a Foster Grant advertisement published in *Modern Plastics* magazine, April, 1969.

Now, since God has sent a few "earth quakes and April showers" into our life, we're becoming more like His Son.

His plan is working! We're becoming more mature and taking more "leading roles" on the stage of life. But we don't want to "let the curtain drop here." There are others out there, who can't go on in their old lifestyle.

Let's help them "get their act together," so they can perform a more dedicated role.*

woodpeckers." The North Vietnamese never mastered the code, which laid out the alphabet on a simple 5-by-5 grid (omitting K, for which C was used). They tapped first the line, then the letter in that line. Thus the letter B would be tap——tap-tap.

The code flowed so fluently that the men told one another jokes. Kicks on the wall meant a laugh! Every Sunday, at a coded signal, the men stood and recited the Lord's Prayer and the Pledge of Allegiance.[1]

Communicating to one another is a part of life. Communicating truth and living out that truth gives direction and meaning to life.

During your lifetime, who has influenced you more than anyone else? What was it about that individual that caused you to learn from them? Often the answer to that question is: "That person believed in me." "They stuck with me." "They saw potential in me." Larry Crabb says, "I could trust a person who delighted in me."[2]

You are designed to be that person to your study group? Communicate the truth in love, acknowledging their worth, and express your expectations for their success in living out truth in their journey.

> **Great leaders with great teams** *produce great moments in our lives—the Michael Jordan Chicago Bulls, the Roger Staubach Dallas Cowboys, the Payne Stewart 1999 Ryder Cup. All these threw excitement into our daily routine. The focus on purpose, the blending of abilities, the endurance through crisis—victory is the sweet result of a team that jells.*[3]

As you look back over your life, some of your greatest moments have come because you were part of a team that held together and won. But did you realize that the most important team you will ever play on was formed the moment you put your trust in Christ Jesus as your only way to heaven? And the greatest threat to the unity and victory of this team is the failure to learn and follow truth!

> *"To look is one thing. To see what you look at is another. To understand what you see is a third. To learn from what you understand is still something else. But to act on what you learn is what really matters"*[4]

Our desire is to dedicate ourselves and to encourage others to be willing to look at Biblical truth, to understand its meaning, to learn how that applies to our personal lives and to act on what we learn.

> Spiritual growth is developmental—progressively learned, building block by building block, slowly over time. The process is a journey, a pilgrimage through the unknown valleys of trial, tempest, and turmoil.[5]

The journey itself is a preparation where each experience is cumulatively used to prepare our hearts for the next turn in the road.[6]

May God richly bless you as you guide others on this journey, in light of His soon return.

DEDICATION

Chapter 1

Leader's Prayer

Pray that each member of the study group will be challenged to become (by His grace) a more dedicated follower of Jesus Christ.

Leader's Plan

Share with the group what Christ means in your life **now**, and how you pray that He may use you in an ever increasing way as the weeks and months and years go by.

Express your heart to them, they will benefit from knowing you and your **dedication**.

"He died for all, that they who live should no longer live for themselves, but for Him who died and rose again on their behalf."

II Corinthians 5:15

I*n 1909, San Francisco was recovering from the great earthquake. At the same time, the Dockstader Minstrels, who were appearing there, encountered an earth-shaking problem of their own.*

Charlie Zeffler, one of their star performers broke his ankle. As Lew Dockstader, the director of the entertainment group was considering how he could replace his star performer, he decided on a little-known substitute to go on in his place.

That evening, as the stand-in singer was ending his final song, he fell to his knees and, putting his heart into the performance, he sang, "…I'd walk a million miles for just one of your smiles, my Maa-aa-amm-my."

Much like the great earthquake, the applause shook the rafters. It was then, at that moment, that Al Jolson, the greatest entertainer in the world, was introduced to the world. Everywhere he would go, he touched the hearts of thousands with songs like "Swanee," "April Showers," and "Sonny-Boy." Jolson's emotional technique was so overwhelming that grown men would shed tears as he sang. And hardened men would leave the performance to send a letter to their mothers.[1]

This reminds us a bit of our own JOURNEY. When we were just getting started in our walk with Christ, we felt that within the Christian community we didn't have much of an opportunity to be a "part of the act." And not knowing a great deal about Scripture, we figured that there was very little demand for our "song and dance." The more mature believers seemed

Note

"You ain't heard nothin' yet" is a phrase that Al Jolson made famous in the first talkie movie, The Jazz Singer, in 1928.

Note

Ephesians 2:8-9 has just explained that eternal life came to us as a gift of God. It came by *grace* which is God's great goodness given to utterly undeserving people.[2] **Everyone who has put their trust in Christ alone for eternal life must be reminded that we are beneficiaries of this grace. That was God's gift to a <u>guilty sinner</u>.**

But now, here in Ephesians 2:10 we see the special work that God has for a <u>loyal disciple</u>.[3]

- Ephesians 2:8-9 is all about life without end to anyone who will simply believe Christ for it. It's a **gift**.

- Ephesians 2:10 is all about rewards and great joy to all who will dedicate their lives to the work that God has prepared for us to accomplish. This involves **work**.

to have their "act all together," so assuming that there was no part for an amateur at the moment, we just "waited in the wings for our cue."*

Now, since God has sent a few "earth quakes and April showers" into our life, we're becoming more like His Son. His plan is working! We're becoming more mature and taking more "leading roles" on the stage of life. But we don't want to "let the curtain drop here."

There are others out there, who can't go on in their old lifestyle. Let's help them "get their act together," so they can perform a more dedicated role.

"They ain't heard nothin' yet."

Once We are Saved, God has a <u>Purpose</u> for our Life

Like Al Jolson, we need to be dedicated, but our dedication is to develop our skills in living out our godly character from day to day.

> *"For we are His workmanship, created in Christ Jesus for good works, which God prepared beforehand, that we should walk in them."*
>
> Ephesians 2:10

The term "**workmanship**" means that we are His "creation." He has "made" us. Much like a potter, as a skilled craftsman, molds and shapes clay into a special shape and decorates its surface with special knives and brushes, we are fashioned by God, Himself. This is what happened to every person who is saved by grace. We are a new creation, the product of the skill and craftsmanship of God.

Every vessel created by a human craftsman has a special use and purpose for which it was designed.[4] Some vessels were crafted to be used in storing valuable supplies; others were made for transporting; while still others were especially fashioned to withstand extremely hot temperatures necessary for preparing food or purifying precious metals. The same is true of each of us who are the "workmanship" of our Creator and Savior.

Ephesians 2:10 says that we were "...**created** ...**for good words**." This is the purpose for which we were made. God created us for the function of doing good things. That's how our life after we are saved should be characterized.

This verse also says that the good works that we were created to do were things that "...**God prepared beforehand**." That means that He prepared things for us to accomplish ahead of time.

✦ The believer is designed for the **work**.

✦ And the work is designed for the **believer**.[5]

Every believer is created this way. At the end of our lives we will all have a story to tell. The story will be the drama of our life. It will be about the thoughts that we allow to shape our decisions; our actions, and our words. We'll all look back some day and either be extremely glad that we fulfilled the purpose for which God created us or excruciatingly sad that we were not passionate about good things we were created to do.

> *Robert Frayser, a 47-year-old Kansas doctor, was overcome by carbon monoxide from a leaking exhaust system in his single-engine plane. He blacked out after flying about 100 miles from Kansas to Missouri. Frayser woke up more than 250 miles later after the plane, on autopilot, ran out of gas and landed in a Moberly, Missouri field.*[6]

As believers, who have not yet learned how special we are to our Creator, we are all prone to be like this pilot in a sense. We are unconscious to the direction our lives are heading and hoping for the best at the end of our destination. Please, take a word of warning. Take your life off of autopilot and make wise decisions now in the early part of your *JOURNEY*.

If we allow Him to do so, God will develop our skill and knowledge, so that we can glorify Him in accomplishing what He has created us to do. We should dedicate ourselves to learning all that Christ wants us to **know**; in order to become all that He wants us to **be**; in order to accomplish all that He created us to **do**.[7]

Ted Engstrom in *The Pursuit of Excellence* writes:

> *"**I was cleaning** out a desk drawer when I found a flashlight I hadn't used in over a year. I flipped the switch but wasn't surprised when it gave no light. I unscrewed it and shook it to get the batteries out, but they wouldn't budge. Finally, after some effort, they came loose. What a mess! Battery acid had*

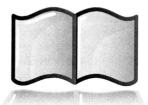

Memory Verse
Ephesians 2:10

Comment

"In John 9:5, Jesus said, *"While I am in the world, I am the **light** of the world."*

Now, of course, Jesus is at the right hand of the Father, and we are here as His representatives. Regarding our responsibility, Jesus said in Matthew 5:14, 16, *"You are the light of the world...Let your light shine before men in such a way, that they may see your good works, and glorify your Father who is in heaven."*

It is clear that we were created to be lights in this present world, where people are walking in darkness. Paul told the Philippians: *"Do all things without grumbling and disputing; that you may prove yourselves to be blameless and innocent, children of God, above reproach in the midst of a crooked and perverse generation, among whom you appear as **lights** in the world, holding forth the Word of Life."* (2:14-16a)

To the Ephesians he wrote: *"...you were formerly in darkness, but now you are **light** in the world; walk as children of **light**."* (5:8)

And he explained to the Corinthians: *"For we do not preach ourselves but Christ Jesus as Lord, and ourselves as your bond-servants for Jesus' sake. For God, who said, '**Light** shall shine out of darkness', is the One who has shone in our hearts to give the **light** of the knowledge of the glory of God in the face of Christ."* (4:5-6)

The message was clearly taught in the early church that we are to outwardly speak forth the light of the knowledge of Christ. If we keep quiet, how will others hear the story about Jesus Christ?

corroded the entire inside of the flashlight. The batteries were new when I'd put them in, and I'd stored them in a safe, warm place. But there was one problem. Those batteries weren't made to be warm and comfortable. They were designed to be turned on—to be used. That's the same with us. We weren't created to be warm, safe, and comfortable. You and I were made to be 'turned on'...to let our light shine."[8]

Be Who God Made You To Be
(Imitate~Don't Impersonate)

When Scripture tells us to "let our light shine," that means that we are to live openly and visibly in this world as representatives of Christ. We are to be like Him and tell others about Him—we are not to *impersonate* Him, but rather we are to *imitate* Him. No one can be God. But we are to be *like* God in character, and give the message about what He has done for us. *We can be ourselves* and live out *His* character and tell *His* message.

> **When Elvis Presley died**, there were 48 professional Elvis impersonators. In 1996, there were 7,328. What will happen if this rate of growth continues? By the year 2012, one out of every four people on the face of the earth will be an Elvis impersonator!!! Now, that's something to get you all shook up![9]

This world doesn't need any more impersonators. We need believers to become who we were created to be. God will use our lives in a greater way than we can imagine.

Todd Beamer (a hero in the Sept. 11, 2001 terrorist attack) is well established in our American history—and the story of his life and beliefs are now a part of Russian history:

> **After seeing** Todd's wife, Lisa, interviewed on national television, a group of Russian reporters flew over for an interview of their own. Lisa Beamer invited the Russians to Princeton Alliance Church in New Jersey and showed them the classroom where Todd taught Sunday School.
>
> On the marker board was a diagram depicting the chasm between God's holiness and man's sinfulness. A cross was

drawn to symbolize the bridge which was created by Christ's sacrificial death. Eugene, a Russian bureau chief, said he had never seen anything like this and wanted to know more. After further explanation, he put his trust in Jesus Christ. Eugene returned to Russia and prepared a news broadcast about the Beamers that included the bridge diagram.[10]

Now millions of Russians have heard the gospel because a brave young widow, like her brave husband, was willing to shine. And now, a new believer by the name of Eugene is turned on and shining in Russia—fulfilling the purpose for which he also was created.

There's a Lead <u>Role</u> for You to Play

There is an incredible need for dedicated Christians to take a serious role in influencing their world for Christ.

I realize that people who are unconcerned about being a light, or making a difference in this world are difficult to motivate. However, if you are concerned, and you are only holding off because you are inexperienced or just plain frightened, I've got some information that you will want to know.

Since we are *"His workmanship,"* we are not just a creation, we are a **masterpiece**. God doesn't make anything of poor quality. Tony Evans points out that a masterpiece is identified by the artist who created it. You always identify the art by the artist.[13] For example, when you are discussing paintings, people will say, *"Oh, that's a Da Vinci."* Or if you are talking about music, you'll hear the phrase, *"That's Handel's Messiah."*

The reason we have great pieces of art is because we had great artists.[14] All believers are "created in Christ" we are identified as "Christians." We are His masterpiece—each one of us was created for a special purpose.

Since we are identified by His name, then when we are at work or at school or at home, people there ought to see our character and our activities and our language and say, **"Christ Jesus sure can create a masterpiece!"**

Now, just to put what we have said in perspective, allow me to say that we are a masterpiece that God is still working on. Our story is the story of **transformation**. You will not always be the same as you are today.[15] God loves you and is involved even now in making you more perfectly what you are intended in His plan to become.

"Workmanship"

"to make or create" This is used of works of divine creation.[15]

"Transformed"
This refers to "a transformation that is invisible to the physical eye."[19]

The word here is **metamorphoo**. From this we get our English word **metamorphosis**, which describes how a caterpillar is transformed into a butterfly.

The change that we undergo as dedicated followers of Christ will be more wonderful than a caterpillar turning into a butterfly.[20]

This term is used in Romans 12:1-2 and II Corinthians 3:18.

"I've missed more than 9,000 shots in my career. I've lost almost 300 games. Twenty-six times I've been trusted to take the game-winning shot and missed. I've failed over and over again in my life. And that is why I succeed."

Michael Jordan

At the sight of the destruction of the two towers of the world trade center, high above the skyline of Ground Zero are hidden 35-millimeter cameras that are capturing all of the activity through time-lapse photography. Three cameras were installed on top of nearby buildings in May of 2002 and three more were installed by September 11, 2002. Each camera is programmed to take a picture of the 16-acre sight every five minutes for the next seven years. Those in charge of the project plan to create a historic record of the rebirth of the World Trade Center site. With over four million pictures from which to work, they are hoping the finished product will be displayed at a museum on the site itself. The purpose of these cameras are not to chronicle the tragedy, but the **transformation**. *The sponsors believe something great will be created.*[16]

God plans the same kind of transformation for each of us.

As long as He is running the show, we can be sure our performance will continue to improve. In the eyes of the world, we might not be very impressive, yet, but hang in there because, for the work that God has designed for you, you are His choice.

In the National Basketball Association draft of 1984, the Houston Rockets had the number **one** *pick. They opted for Akeem Olajuwon who led them to two consecutive NBA championships in 1994 and 1995. The Portland Trailblazers took Samuel Bowie as the number* **two** *draft pick for that year. Unfortunately, Bowie was injured and did not reach the potential for which Portland had hoped. The Chicago Bulls had the* **third** *pick, and they selected a young man who was* passed over *by both Houston and Portland. It was none other than Michael Jordan, the round-ball legend who took his team to the top of the basketball world in 1991, 1992, 1993, 1996, 1997, and 1998. Ironically the two years that Houston won was during Jordan's stint in baseball. Speculative historians can only imagine what would have happened had Jordan not taken a sabbatical in 1994 and 1995, or retired after the championship in 1998.*[17]

The Bible tells about another lad who was involved in a draft that held some surprising similarities.[18] Samuel had the responsibility of anointing a new king for Israel (I Samuel 16). Those who seemed to be the best candidates (in man's opinion) didn't get the job, and Samuel, under God's guidance chose the one, that, to the world seemed less likely. Through faithfulness in many experiences of his life, David was transformed by God into a great warrior and king.

Tony Evans says that when he was growing up, one of his favorite TV programs was Superman. He says,

> **"I loved to see Superman** because I loved the contrast. Here he was, Clark Kent, a nobody. People would push him around, beat him up, and laugh at him. He was always tripping and stumbling. Ooh, but don't let him get near a telephone booth!

> Because, when this man went into a telephone booth, something happened. All of a sudden his jacket came off. He would take off his glasses and loosen his tie. And the kids would go, "Uh, oh!"

> That meant that the enemy was in trouble. The guys around Metropolis, who were causing all the havoc, were in for a bad time.

> Why? Because, bustin' out of the telephone booth, now was a man with a red and blue suit and a cape that had an "S" on his chest. **Superman!**

> All of a sudden, this nobody became a hero, feared by criminals and respected by the citizens—a man, who could grab speeding bullets; out run locomotives; jump over buildings, and fly along side of planes. He could do whatever was supernaturally needed.

> Although he was Clark Kent on the outside, whenever something went wrong that some more power was needed, he knew the telephone booth was right around the corner."[21]

That telephone booth can represent the transforming power of God's Word and His grace. Without it we are all spiritual Clark Kents, bumbling failures,[22] but when we go into the telephone booth of dedication, and, in

"Perfection is not attainable, but in chasing it you could catch excellence."
Vince Lombardi

"Never let the fear of striking out get in your way."
Babe Ruth

Contrast
Salvation is a free gift, received by faith alone in Christ. The believer is secure in his position of eternal life from the moment of saving faith because of the faithfulness of God.

Discipleship requires the costly commitment of a believer's life, expressed through steadfast obedience to Jesus Christ. The enduring disciple is promised special rewards in Christ's future Kingdom because of his faithfulness to God.

Discipleship

In his book, *God's Glorious Church*, Tony Evans explains:

*"**Disciple**" is not a uniquely Christian term. It means "student or learner." The Greeks, under Aristotle established schools to train disciples in their way of thinking (philosophy).*

Their discipleship system was very effective. Even after Rome conquered Greece, the Romans could not eradicate Greek influence. So While Rome held military power, the Greeks continued to hold power over the culture, because of well-trained Greek disciples.

These people lived under Roman rule, but their thinking was Greek, and in the end, what people think is a lot more important than what an external power can force them to do.

*This helps us understand why Jesus commissioned the church to "**make disciples**." When it's done right, the disciple becomes a follower for life.*

The real battle for souls is waged in the mind. A well-trained disciple can live in a foreign, hostile culture without succumbing to that culture because his mind is fixed on another world.

God's Glorious Church, p. 57

prayer, humble ourselves in obedience to God's guiding Word, we are transformed into someone much closer to who He made us to be. Ordinary people can experience extraordinary change.[23] People like you and I can do extraordinary things.

Charles Colson, in *Loving God*, tells the story of Telemachus, a fourth-century Christian.

> **He lived in a remote village**, *tending his garden and spending much of his time in prayer. …He traveled to Rome on foot and happened to be in the city at the time of a great festival. The little monk followed the crowd surging down the streets into the Coliseum. He saw the gladiators stand before the emperor and say, "We, who are about to die, salute you." Then he realized these men were going to fight to the death for the entertainment of the crowd…He cried out, "In the name of Christ, stop!"*
>
> *As the games began, he pushed his way through the crowd, climbed over the wall, and dropped to the floor of the arena. When the crowd saw this tiny figure rushing to the gladiators and saying, "In the name of Christ, stop!," they thought it was part of the show and began laughing.*
>
> *When they realized it wasn't, the laughter turned to anger. As he was pleading with the gladiators to stop, one of them plunged a sword into his body. He fell to the sand. As he was dying, his last words were, "In the name of Christ, stop."*
>
> *Then a strange thing happened. The gladiators stood looking at the tiny figure lying there. A hush fell over the coliseum. Way up in the upper rows, a man stood and made his way to the exit. Others began to follow. In dead silence, everyone left the coliseum. The year was A.D. 391, and that was the last battle to the death between gladiators in the Roman Coliseum. Never again in the great stadium did men kill each other for the entertainment of the crowd, all because of one tiny voice that could hardly be heard above the tumult. One voice—one life—that spoke the truth in God's name."*[24]

We need to determine to step up to the plate. Give God a chance to show what He can accomplish through you.

Bob Richards, Olympic gold medal winner, said,

> **Five million people** *could have beaten me in the pole vault the years I won it—men, who were stronger, bigger, and faster, but they never picked up a pole. There are many people who could have been Olympic champions, but they have never tried."*[25]

If we could only get a glimpse at our potential. Our beginning steps of a life dedicated to Christ might seem small, even insignificant. But if you seem to be having difficulty getting started, just consider this.

> **After their futile attempts to fly** *at Kitty Hawk in 1901, Wilbur confessed to his younger brother that "men would not fly for 50 years."*
>
> *But just two years later, they not only flew their experimental plane, they flew it at 31 miles per hour. Just 44 years later, Chuck Yeager flew faster than the speed of sound. Within 65 years, man flew to the moon. When John Glenn boarded the Space Shuttle Discovery in 1998, he took a small piece of wing fabric from the plane flown at Kitty Hawk, and that 95-year-old piece of cloth orbited the earth at 17,500 mph.*[26]

Never underestimate our potential in Christ. The Almighty God indwells us, and it is He who is "…at work in you, both to will and to work for His good pleasure." (Philippians 2:13)

Dedication should be done in the Days of our <u>Youth</u>

It matters a tremendous amount who sits in the director's chair of our life. An equally important truth is that dedication should be in the days of our youth. "Why is that true?" Because our lives become very cluttered—filled with so many plans and goals that have nothing to do with the things that God has prepared for us.

> **A seminar leader** *introduced the audience to a wide-mouth gallon jar. He then showed them some fist-size rocks and asked them to guess how many rocks would fit in the jar. The audience made their guesses as he filled up the jar with those large rocks. He then asked, "Is the container full?" They looked at*

Looking back on your life with Christ, can you see some transformation that God has accomplished in you?

Salvation

1. A once-and-for-all single event with lasting results

2. A free gift (it cost man nothing)

3. The crediting to our account the righteousness of God

4. This is God's workmanship

5. Assures man's entrance into heaven

Discipleship

1. Doing the will of God as a daily, continuing commitment

2. Very costly (sometimes even our life)

3. Developing a personal righteousness based on good works

4. Fulfills the purpose for which God created us

5. Assures that you will receive rewards in heaven[11]

the jar-full of rocks and replied, "Yes." He smiled, then pulled out some gravel and began pouring it into the jar until it reached the rim. He again asked, "Is it full?" This time the listeners were thinking differently. They replied, "Probably not."

He affirmed their response while reaching for some sand. Once the sand came to the top, his question returned, "Is it full?" By now the audience was in tune with the ploy. They shouted, "No!" He smiled and began pouring water until the jar was filled to the brim. Then he asked "**What's the point?**" Someone instantly said, "Well, there are gaps, and if you really work at it, you can always fit more into your life." The reply was rather stern, "No. That's not the point. The point is this: If you hadn't put these big rocks in **first**, you would have never gotten them in."[27]

If we do not give our greatest attention to the most important decisions (the big things in our life) and make them our highest priority, then something of lesser importance will very quickly take their place, and fill up all of the time spaces in our life.[28] Put the big rocks in first!

In Psalm 71:5 the psalmist says,

> **"For Thou art my hope; O Lord God, Thou art my confidence from my <u>youth</u>."**

Solomon says in Ecclesiastes 12:1

> **"Remember also your Creator in the days of your <u>youth</u>."**

We are told in II Peter 3:18 to:

> **"...grow in the grace and knowledge of our Lord and Savior Jesus Christ. To Him be glory, both <u>now</u> and to the day of eternity..."**

If we are to "**grow**" it makes sense to start when we are young enough to accomplish more growth. All of our Olympic athletes begin training when they are very young. Our great musicians and entertainers dedicate themselves to grow in their abilities at a very early age. Don't let less important things take your time and life away.

Walt Disney was ruthless in cutting anything that got in the way of a story's pacing. Ward Kimball, one of the animators for Snow White, *recalls working 240 days on a 4-1/2 minute sequence in which the dwarfs made soup for Snow White and almost destroyed the kitchen in the process. Disney thought it was funny, but he decided the scene stopped the flow of the picture, so out it went.*[29]

When the film of our lives is shown, will it be as great as it might be.[30] A lot will depend on the multitude of "good" things we need to eliminate to make way for the great things God has prepared for us to do.

It is necessary, at times to leave out some good things in order to accomplish the best things. That's what dedication is about.

> *Seven whales died on the Baha Peninsula. They were beached. People couldn't get them back into the water. When the local newspaper wrote up the tragic story, the headlines read:* **"Giants Perish While Chasing Minnows."**

So, when we look down the road to where we want to be years from now (a person of mature, responsible, reliable, well-developed character) there are some extremely difficult but very necessary changes that we must make now in order to end up where we need to be as fully **dedicated** followers of Christ.

> *For many years, I can remember seeing the television program called* The Wide World of Sports. *That sports program would always open with an awesome illustration of "the agony of defeat." It would show the painful ending of an attempted ski jump. The skier appeared in good form as he headed down the jump, but then, for no apparent reason, he tumbled head over heels off the side of the jump ramp, bouncing off the supporting structure.*
>
> *What the TV viewers didn't know was that he chose to fall rather than finish the jump. Why? As he explained later, the jump surface had become too fast, and midway down the ramp, he realized that if he completed the jump, he would land on the level ground, beyond the safe sloping landing area, which could have been fatal.*

Great military leaders have said that all you have to do to defeat an enemy is to **distract** him.

- *"But you, O man of God, <u>flee</u> these things (see context, v. 9, 10) and pursue righteousness, godliness, faith, love, perseverance and gentleness."* (I Timothy 6:11)

- *"Now <u>flee</u> from youthful lusts, and pursue righteousness, faith, love and peace, with those who call on the Lord from a pure heart."* (II Timothy 2:22)

- *"<u>Flee</u> immorality. Every other sin that a man commits is outside the body, but the immoral man sins against his own body."* (I Corinthians 6:18)

- *"Therefore, my beloved, <u>flee</u> from idolatry."* (see the context of verses 11-13)

- *"Therefore, since we have so great a cloud of witnesses surrounding us, let us also <u>lay aside every encumbrance, and the sin which so easily entangles us</u>, and let us run with endurance the race that is set before us."* (Hebrews 12:1)

- *"And <u>do not be conformed to this world</u>, but be transformed by the renewing of your mind…"* (Romans 12:2a)

As it was, the skier suffered no more than a headache from the tumble.[31]

To change our course in life can be dramatic and sometimes extremely painful, but change is better than a fatal landing at the end of the ramp.[32] The change you have to make can include thoughts and practices that you are aware of as being sin. Taking inventory of our life and changing things (with God's strength) while we still have time, is wise. We're all required to make some adjustments for optimum effectiveness in God's Kingdom. We will, no doubt have to change some good habits as well. Things that, of themselves, are not bad, but just not helpful in achieving serious dedication. And yet, we must evaluate things that are absolutely necessary for reaching our goal. The better choices that we have made and that we are fully aware of as being pleasing to God, these very useful aspects of our life—must be guarded.

Hold on to them! Never let go!

On a flight from Portland, Maine to Boston, *Henry Dempsey, the pilot, heard an unusual noise near the rear of the small plane. He asked his co-pilot to take over the controls and went to check it out.*

As he made his way to the tail section, the plane hit an air pocket, and Dempsey was slammed against the rear door. The door, which had not been properly latched prior to the takeoff, flew open and he was instantly sucked out of the jet.

The co-pilot, seeing the red light, which indicates an open door, radioed the nearest airport, requesting permission to make an emergency landing. He reported the loss of the pilot and called for a helicopter search of that area of the ocean.

After the plane landed, they found Henry Dempsey— holding on to the outdoor ladder of the aircraft. Somehow he had caught the ladder, held on for 10 minutes as the jet flew 200 mph at an altitude of 4,000 feet. At landing, he kept his head from hitting the runway, which was only 12 inches away. It took the rescue personnel several minutes to pry Dempsey's fingers from the ladder.[33]

That man found something worth holding on to! Here in this world, life can get pretty turbulent, and holding on can become so difficult, but we must consider the alternative!

The Disciples Commitment to Dedication <u>Grew</u> More and More as They <u>Continued</u> to Follow Christ

The disciples commitment to dedication grew more and more as they continued to follow Christ.

Let's look at three different occasions when the disciples grew in their knowledge of Jesus and in their level of dedication to Him.

Phase #1 of Their Journey: Matthew 4:18-22

(Turn to this reference and ask someone to read the narrative.)

This scene, described by Matthew at the Sea of Galilee is not the same as that described in John 1:35-42 (that was when the disciples first met Jesus.) Here, John the Baptist is not with them, as he had already been taken into custody. (Read also this event in Mark 1:14-20.)

By this time, they had already put their trust in Jesus (John 2:11). As Jesus says to them, *"Follow Me."* He speaks of a change that will take place in their lives: *"I will make you to become fishers of men."* (Matthew 4:19)

Here, dedication is easily observed, as we see the disciples *"left their nets and followed Him"* (v. 20) and *"left their boat and father"* (v. 22).

Phase #2 of Their Journey: Luke 5:1-11

(Turn to this reference and ask someone to read the narrative.)

Later on in their *JOURNEY*, after Jesus had healed many people, including Peter's mother-in-law, the disciples came again to the Sea of Galilee.

At this point in the spiritual development of the disciples, they were made more aware of the awesome greatness of our Lord, as He shows that He is able to cause them to catch great multitudes of fish.

Here Jesus moves from the promise He made back in Matthew 4 (that He would (future) make them fishers of men) to a present fulfillment when He says, *"From now on you will catch men."* (v. 10)

Concept

Dedication involves both changing some things that will hold us back and holding on to the things that will help us reach our goal.

Note

"Lake of Gennesaret"

Luke is the only one who calls this body of water a "lake." Matthew and Mark call it the Sea of Galilee, and John calls it the Sea of Tiberias.

Here are some verses which express the concept of holding on to the good things that will help us become more fully dedicated.

Have the study group turn to each verse in their Bibles. They could also list the topic: **Dedication** in a clear page in the back of their Bibles and make a list of these verse references.

- *"Take hold of instruction; and do not let go. Guard her, for she is your life."* (Proverbs 4:13)

- *"But examine everything carefully; hold fast to that which is good."* (I Thessalonians 5:21)

- *"So then, brethren, stand firm and hold to the teachings we passed on to you, whether by word of mouth or by letter."* (II Thessalonians 2:15d)

- *"Hold fast the form of sound words, which you have heard of me, in faith and love which is in Christ Jesus."* (II Timothy 1:13)

Here the disciples had arrived at an even deeper stage of **dedication** to the Lord Jesus, as they *"**left everything** and followed Him."*

They are now comprehending more fully who He is, and what power He possesses. As a result, we see worship and obedience.

Phase #3 of Their Journey: Matthew 16:13-28

(Turn to this reference and ask someone to read the narrative.)

After the feeding of the five thousand and after Jesus walks on the Sea of Galilee, during the violent storm, they traveled to Caesaera Philippi. It is at this location in their *JOURNEY* that they learned about the cost involved in more serious **dedication**.

Up until now, they had not comprehended the future suffering that would occur. In verses 24 through 28, Jesus teaches them what submission to God's will is about in a much deeper sense.

*"**If anyone desires to come after Me, let him deny himself, and take up his cross and follow Me.**"*

This is the cost of greater dedication. Remember that discipleship is a progression. As we walk with Jesus Christ in loyalty to Him, we are gradually transformed. It is a journey of continuing maturity and increasing commitment to be ready at an instant to imitate Christ in our "performance." Like Al Jolson, if you are called on for a sudden performance on the stage of life and ministry, that's when your personal dedication will really show up. It will be your time to let others see what a difference the Lord has made in your life.

Amazing Grace *is more than a song, it's the personal story about the transformation of John Newton. His mother taught him the Bible and prayed for him diligently, but she died before his seventh birthday. By age eleven, Newton's father took him out of boarding school and brought him aboard the merchant ship he captained. He began to acquire a profane education. His total rebellion and disregard for authority led to his father's having to force him into the Royal Navy. Ultimately, he became involved in slave trading. His wickedness* *knew no limits. He enjoyed encountering Christians and trying to undermine and destroy their faith. He referred to himself as an "unrestrained blasphemer."*

But that all changed when God captured his attention in a furious storm (probably an answer to his mother's prayers). His ship was battered for four weeks by the harsh elements off the coast of Newfoundland. Numerous holes in the ship had to be plugged with the clothing of crew members. Most of their food was gone and they were freezing in the cold North Atlantic weather. Through God's mercy, the cargo of beeswax and wood, both lighter than water, helped keep their ship from sinking.

Newton found a copy of The Imitation of Christ *by Thomas Kempis and began to wonder about his eternity. His hopeless situation on an imperiled ship seemed to mirror his destructive life. It was then that he pleaded to God for His mercy and received God's Amazing Grace. His ship was miraculously saved and brought safely to harbor. Transformation took hold of Newton as he studied God's Word faithfully. He withdrew from slave trading and became a minister for the final forty-three years of his life. His ministry influenced the life of William Carey. He also influenced William Wilberforce in his work to abolish slavery in Britain.*

Newton wrote 280 hymns but he is remembered most for the one that describes his life. His transformation is summarized by the words which were placed on his tombstone when he died in 1807: "John Newton, once an infidel and libertine, a servant of slaves in Africa, was, by the rich mercy of our Lord and Savior Jesus Christ, preserved, restored, pardoned, and appointed to preach the faith he had long labored to destroy."[34]

His power to transform is absolutely amazing. And the longer we faithfully follow Him the more we'll be conformed to His image. That's the plan and the purpose for the JOURNEY.

The quality of our adult Christian life is determined by the decisions and habits of our youth.[35] Though we may be unaware of the powerful impact of our early years, they are the foundation of our later years.

Can you recall events in your life that reveal a more increasing dedication to Christ as your walk with Him continues?

Illustration

"By faith we understand that the worlds were framed by the Word of God, so that the things which are seen were not made of things which do appear." (Hebrews 11:3)

If we traveled at the speed of light (186,000 miles per second) it would take us 100,000 years to travel across the diameter of the Milky Way. There are several hundred billion galaxies like the Milky Way. Our mind can hardly comprehend the size of the universe. And if God created the universe by His Word, then what can His Word do in my life?[36]

At a time in history before the invention of powerful telescopes, it was supposed that the universe was rather small. During those times it seemed easy to see man as having a great deal of importance in God's creation.

But in the late 18th century we learned that our universe is 20 billion light years in diameter. Knowing that we are located on the edge of a minor galaxy among billions of larger galaxies caused man to lose his sense of significance.

Then when we turn in God's Word and read about His plan for us to rule over this vast created order, our importance is much greater than we had once thought.

Instead of being created to rule a small planet, dedicated followers are destined to subdue the universe and rule over the galaxies.[37]

"What is man, that Thou dost take thought of him? And the son of man that Thou dost care for him? Yet Thou hast made him a little lower than God, and dost crown him with glory and majesty! Thou dost make him to rule over the works of Thy hands. Thou hast put all things under his feet."

Psalm 8:4-6

Have you ever received a gift or made a purchase that you had to do "some assembly required"? I don't know about you, but when I "assemble" anything, I inevitably have parts left over. Parts that seem to have no role to play. Makes you think that someone at the factory puts in some spare parts.

It might encourage you to know that this is not how God works. He does not make spare parts.[38] You are not a left over; you have a role to play. God has a specific purpose for you that is central to His plan. **Dedicated** believers have lived and are now with Christ. Others, who will also be dedicated to an awesome performance will come on the scene after you. But God has created you for today.

If this generation hears the truth of the gospel and observes a life that is genuine, it will be because of you. This is your day. So, get ready friend. **It's show time!**

> **"O God, You have taught me from my youth; and I will declare Your wondrous deeds..."**
>
> Psalm 71:17

DISCIPLESHIP

"Disciple"
Disciple refers to a "pupil, apprentice or adherent" (someone who is learning from an instructor).[1]

"Abide"
Abide means "to continue, remain, or stay."[2]

A Disciple has Responsibilities

A **"Disciple"** is the name which describes those believers who gathered around Jesus to learn from Him as a "pupil." The basic meaning of this word is *"a pupil, apprentice, disciple or adherent."*[1] Discipleship is the believer's journey towards becoming like Christ.

There are some specific responsibilities for a believer to "become" a disciple and to be an "effective" disciple. We will look at three.

First Responsibility: Abide in His Word

(Notice that Jesus is talking to believers.)

> *"As He spoke these things, many came to believe in Him. Jesus therefore was saying to those Jews who had believed Him, 'If you abide in My word, then you are truly <u>disciples</u> of Mine.'"*

John 8:30-31

Jesus desires that all believers choose to become learners. He says that we are to "abide" in His word. The word abide means "to continue or remain or stay."[2] So, here, Jesus is saying that a disciple is one who continues or stays in the teaching of His word.

That happens when, in our daily lives, we apply God's word to the situations we face and the decisions we make. Remaining in His word means to live according to the principles and guidelines recorded in the Bible.

When we do this, our lives are being transformed a little each day. Often we are not aware of all that God is doing as we are involved in this process of being a disciple.

Leader's Prayer
Pray for a desire to be in the heart of every member of your study group to become all that Christ desires us to be.

Pray that, as we learn more about following Christ in close friendship, that this will become the life-goal of each one in your group.

Leader's Plan
Express freely to the group, your opinion of the value of following Christ and learning the valuable skills found in His word.

Convey to them, in your own words, how the present difficulties of this life are not worthy to be compared to the greatness of our blessings in God's Kingdom.

Memory Verse

John 8:31

Note

In the same way the Karate Kid had to practice, we have that concept taught in Hebrews 5:14. We are told there that mature believers "because of practice have their senses trained to discern good and evil."

Sadly, the people who are being spoken to in Hebrews had not practiced and matured as they should. Their description is given in verse 12. "For though by this time you ought to be teachers, you have need again for someone to teach you the elementary principles of the oracles of God, and you have come to need milk and not solid food."

This shows that discipleship is a conditional relationship (teacher and student) that can be interrupted or terminated after it has begun.[4]

The command to "abide" is always referring to an act of the will of the disciple, therefore this shows the disciple that there is a responsibility on his part.[5]

In the movie Karate Kid, *Daniel asks Mr. Miagi to teach him karate. Miagi agrees to teach him under one condition: Daniel must submit to his instruction and not question his methods.*

The next day Daniel shows up eager to learn, but becomes disappointed when Mr. Miagi has him painting a very long fence which extends around his yard. Miagi demonstrates the precise motions for the job: up and down, up and down with each hand. It takes days for Daniel to finish the job.

Next, Miagi has him scrub the deck using a prescribed circle motion. Again the job takes days, and Daniel wonders, "What does this have to do with karate?" But he says nothing.

*Next, Miagi tells Daniel to wash and wax three weather-beaten cars and again prescribes the motion. It is after this third task is finished that Daniel reaches his limit. **"I thought you were going to teach me karate, but all you have done is have me do your unwanted chores."***

*Daniel has broken Miagi's one condition, and the old man becomes very angry. **"I have been teaching you karate! Defend yourself!"***

Maigi thrusts his arm at Daniel, who instinctively defends himself with an arm motion exactly like that used in one of his chores. Miagi unleashes a vicious kick, and again Daniel averts the blow with another motion that had become second nature because of the servant-type work he had been assigned to accomplish. After Daniel successfully defends himself from several more blows, Miagi simply walks away, leaving Daniel to discover what the master had known all along: skill comes from repeating the correct but seemingly mundane actions of life's daily chores.[3]

Daniel was being transformed and did not realize it.

The same is true of discipleship. We should come to Christ with an attitude of unquestioning obedience. He is transforming us into men and women with skills that will be used in representing Him here in our time and also in His Kingdom, which He will establish here in the future. Until then, we must not lose sight of who we are. If we are to become dedicated disciples, we must be *"abiding in His word."*

The second responsibility of a disciple involves a new command:

Second Responsibility: Love One Another

"A new commandment I give to you, that you love one another; as I have loved you, that you also love one another. By this all men will know that you are My <u>disciples</u>, if you have <u>love</u> for one another."

John 13:34-35

The purpose for this second responsibility of a disciple is that we could be *identified* as people who are obediently following Christ.

Notice that Jesus is not saying that by our love for one another, all men will know that we are Christians. Here, He is speaking of discipleship. Jesus is speaking about the most mature spiritual character quality—love. And He says that the purpose of our obedience to His command to *"love one another"* is to create a compelling testimony to the world.[22] Your life is a production. You're on stage.

Love will make the difference in your performance!

> *I recently heard about an unusual ending to an Easter production at a local church. The final scene was about the Ascension of our Lord. The actor who was playing the part of Jesus, was hoisted through an opening in the ceiling, by several stage hands. Everything went as planned until midway through the flight. The guys backstage lost their grip and the Ascension began to look like the Second Coming. As the actor dropped almost all the way back down to the stage, he looked at the surprised audience and said, "Oh, and one more thing. Love one another." The stage hands then lifted him back through the opening in the ceiling.*

Well, I don't know in which church that took place, but it emphasizes the point that our love for one another was not an after thought or a quickly thought up line to save the day. It is the very character of God. It is the way dedicated followers are identified.

Other Scripture

Joshua 1:8 and Psalm 1:2 are good examples of abiding in God's Word.

The students can reference these two Scriptures in the margin beside of John 8:31, and reference John 8:31 beside of the two Old Testament Scriptures.

Concept

Christ is transforming believers into skillful men and women of character, who will represent Him. This is being accomplished as we apply biblical principles to every day life experiences, believing that Christ knows what He is doing and has our best interest at heart.

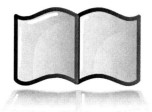

Memory Verse
John 13:35

God Set The Standard For Love

"This is how God showed His love among us: He sent His one and only Son into the world that we might live through Him."

I John 4:9

A high standard for love can easily be drawn from the information that John gives in this famous verse. The kind of love that God wants us to have for one another looks like this:

✦ Love **can be seen**—"...God *showed* His love..."

✦ Love is an **intentional act**—"...He *sent* His one and only Son..."

✦ Love is **costly**—"...His *one and only* Son..."

✦ Love **meets a need**—"...*that we might live* through Him."

*Pick up a bottle of Tabasco sauce. When you read the label, there is a particular word you won't find— "**coloring**." Tabasco sauce is colored naturally by the red peppers from which it is made. The consistency of that color is what makes this story worth telling. During harvest time, workers are sent into the fields with a "**Baton Rouge**." The literal translation of this familiar Louisiana city's namesake is "red stick." Each worker wears a small red stick on their hand which is the size and color of the peppers they are to pick. Only those matching the example are harvested. This stringent standard assures the consistent taste, texture, and color of the 500,000 bottles produced each day at the world's only Tabasco plant located on Avery Island, Louisiana.*

✦ **The written Word is our *standard*.**

✦ **Christ, Himself is our *visible example*.**

Robert Rohm tells the story of the 1961 season of the Green Bay Packers. It was the last game of the year. The Packers had already won enough games to give them the division title before the season was over. Playoffs were two weeks away, and they were about to play the last game of their regular season. It was a not-event type situation, because they could lose and still be in the playoffs.

As the players were getting ready, they were talking about what coach Vince Lombardi was going to say in order to motivate them for such a lack-luster event. The door to Lombardi's office opened. He walked around the dressing room for a short while before he said, "Men, I've been in my office, thinking what to say. Then it dawned on me. If I could go out and play football one more time in my life—If I were younger and stronger—today would be the time I'd choose! You're not playing for Green Bay today. Today, you're playing for your family and friends to show them that you are the champions that they believe you to be—even when you don't have to."

Paul Hornung (the famous halfback for Green Bay) said, "If the dressing room door hadn't been open that day, we'd have run through the wall!"[9]

True Christian love is shown in the same way. It's consistently loving like a champion (disciple) on those lack-luster days, and the non-event type of situations when you're not in church, when the spot light is not on you and when no one is looking.

God's kind of love is shown when we humbly serve one another.

"Having loved His own who were in the world, He now showed them the full extent of His love."

John 13:1 NIV

After Jesus had demonstrated His love for the disciples by humbly washing their feet (an example of loving service), He said to them:

"I have set you an example that you should do as I have done for you."

John 13:15 NIV

Here is a third responsibility that Jesus explained to His disciples. The only unbelieving disciple had removed himself from the group before Jesus' disciple-speech. Judas had gone out from the company of

---

The Standard:
the written Word

The Example:
the incarnate Word

"The real test of love is not that I feel loving, but that others feel loved by me."
Morton Kelsey

Situation—Urgent
In their book *Building A Church of Small Groups*, Bill Donahue and Russ Robinson describe an evening news vignette, which showed police pursuing a government employee who was driving a stolen U.S. Army tank. In that tank at speeds of 40 to 50 miles per hour, he raced through inner-city streets, flattening cars, terrifying pedestrians, smashing into buildings, and toppling traffic signs.

Finally, while trying to cross a major highway, he got hung up on the median wall. Police surrounded the tank and apprehended the suspect. The police worked hard to catch him, because the *stakes were high* and the *situation was urgent*.

What would it look like if we pursued love for other believers with the same urgency? What would it be like if we got serious about following the standard of love that Jesus gave?

Note

The word *"be"* in John 15:8 is the term for *"come into being"* or *"become."*

Therefore, we *"become"* a disciple when we bear <u>much</u> fruit.

Note

The phrase "bear fruit" can refer to:

1. Developing Christian character. *"But the fruit of the Spirit is love, joy, peace, patience, kindness, goodness, faithfulness, gentleness, self-control…"* Galatians 5:22-23

2. This Christian character will produce good actions or good works in our life. *"And we pray this in order that you may live a life worthy of the Lord and may please Him in every way, bearing fruit in every good work…"* Colossians 1:10

3. Bringing other people to Christ through our

(continued on next page)

Jesus and the disciples on the night of the Passover meal, before Jesus washed their feet (John 13:27, 30). Again, note that the instructions are given only to believers.

Third Responsibility: Bear Much Fruit

"Herein is My Father glorified, that ye bear much fruit; so shall ye be My disciples."

John 15:8 KJV

The disciples are told that the Father is glorified if they **"bear much fruit."** (Previously they had been taught *how* "fruit bearing" must be accomplished.) In the first verse of John 15, Jesus explains to the disciples the vital principle for those who are **already "branches."**

Jesus is talking to eleven of the most important men in the history of the church.[6] Since Judas had already gone (John 12:4), there were no unbelievers in the group to whom Jesus was speaking. In 15:3, Jesus tells these men **"You are already clean because of the word which I have spoken to you"** (they are saved) and then He says in verse 4, **"Abide in Me."**

So, we know that John 15 is about Jesus telling men, who are already saved, how to **bear fruit,** and therefore fulfill one of the *responsibilities* of a disciple.

What Does the Phrase "in Me" Mean?

When Jesus uses the phrase *"in Me"* he is referring to maintaining our <u>fellowship</u> with Christ. Fellowship is a very close mutual friendship. This is what He prayed for the disciples in John 17:

"That all of them may be one; as You, Father, are in Me, and I in You, that they also may be in us…"

John 17:21 NIV

Now Jesus would not be referring to the disciples' salvation *"in us"* because they already have that. And He would not give a command in 15:4 to **"Abide in Me"** if that were referring to being saved, because they already were saved, and cannot lose that position. Jesus is saying that the key to bearing fruit (good works) is to **remain in fellowship with Him.** That is the only way we can bear the fruit of good works which we were created in Christ Jesus to do.

> **"Abide" = "to continue, remain, or stay"**
>
> **"in Me" = "fellowship"**

How Do We "Abide in Him"?
(How do we remain in fellowship with Him?)

We "abide" by learning how He wants us to live and by practicing those principles in our daily life. If we are not obedient to His instruction in the Bible, we are not abiding in His fellowship. Look at what Jesus said about this:

"If anyone loves Me, he will obey My teaching. My Father will love him, and we will come to him and make our <u>abode</u> with him."

John 14:23 NIV

Jesus had taught His disciples that obedience to His word would result in Him and His Father "abiding" in their lives. Abiding, then, is based on knowing and keeping the commands of our Lord.[7] Jesus created us for good deeds. He created the deeds for us to accomplish. And He explains that the only way to do them is to remain in fellowship with Him.

(continued from previous page)

witness. *"…you know that the household of Stephanas, that they were the first fruits of Achaia…"* I Corinthians 16:15 (compare Romans 1:13)

4. Giving praise and thanksgiving to God with our lips. *"…let us continually offer up a sacrifice of praise to God, that is, the fruit of lips that give thanks to His name."* Hebrews 13:15

5. Giving of our material resources to be used for the Lord. *"Not that I seek the gift itself, but I seek for the fruit which increases to your account."* Phil. 4:17

(From *So Great Salvation* by Charles C. Ryrie p.45-46)

"Fellowship"
Actual participation or having a share in a close relationship or association with another person[8]

Note

A command (as in 15:4 "*Abide in Me*") cannot refer to a **position** that we already have in Christ.

There would be no need for such a request. The command would have to refer to something that was a choice on the part of the one commanded.

Note

Before that same night was over, all of the disciples ceased to abide in Him. Matthew 26:56 says, "*Then all the disciples forsook Him and fled.*"

Our fellowship with Christ can be restored, as we will see in this next chapter's study. (I John 1:9)

Jesus had spoken these words to Peter in Luke 22:31-32. "*Simon, Simon! Indeed, Satan has asked to have you, that he may sift you as wheat. But I have prayed for you, that your faith should not fail, and when you have turned again, strengthen your brethren.*"

Jesus knew that Peter would lose contact with the True Vine and would need restoration to fellowship.

This is Big! Let's Get it Right.

It is very important (and encouraging) for us to take a close look at John 15:2.

> *"Every branch in Me that does not bear fruit, He takes away; and every branch that bears fruit, He prunes it, that it may bear more fruit."*

John 15:2 NASV

Jesus is describing a believer who:

(1) is *"in Me"*

(2) and *"that does <u>not</u> bear fruit"*

What situations can you think of that would cause an <u>abiding</u> Christian to not bear fruit?

(1) A <u>new</u> Christian, who is just beginning to develop Christ-like character, might be uninformed or not challenged. Remember we are to "<u>grow</u>" in grace and the knowledge of our Lord Jesus Christ.

(2) A Christian, who has <u>suffered a loss</u> of a loved one or a Christian who is battling a <u>long-term illness</u>, might not bear fruit because in situations like this, depression might be a factor.

Special encouragement for believers who are experiencing one or more of the above situations is found in John 15:2. According to Walter Bauer's Greek-English Lexicon (page 24), the word that is translated **"He takes away"** is better translated **"He lifts up."** It is common practice to <u>lift</u> fallen vines with special care, allowing them to begin to heal and gain strength. A weak vine is propped up with a "**Y**" shaped twig. Any dirt or mud is washed off so that the branch again can heal or grow and become productive.

The *JOURNEY* of discipleship is a life-time process. There will be times of fruitfulness as well as times of discouragement. Our needs will be different as we face new situations. The Lord will always be there to help. That's the way His is.

Memo

Every unfruitful Christian, who is yet walking in fellowship, will receive divine encouragement from our heavenly Father.[13]

John chapter 15 is not about going to Heaven or going to Hell. It's about doing something worthwhile with our Christian lives.[13] Jesus is sure the disciples are saved, but He wants them to become fruitful.

Note

The word *"lift up"* is the same word that is translated *"take up."* (**airo**)* This term is used by Jesus in the following passage:

- *"Jesus said to him, 'Arise, take up your pallet, and walk.' And immediately the man became well, and took up his pallet and began to walk."* John 5:8-9

- *"No one has taken it away from Me, but I lay it down on My own initiative. I have authority to lay it down, and I have authority to take it up again…"* John 10:18

Discuss how a new Christian or a Christian who has suffered a great crisis might need to be *"lifted up."* (encouraged and comforted).

*Walter Bauer, *Greek-English Lexicon of the New Testament*, p. 24.

The *responsibilities* of being a disciple are: (1) Abide in His Word (2) Love One Another and (3) Bear Much Fruit. As we abide in Him (remain in His fellowship) and abide in His Word (continue to learn and obey), we will grow stronger and more mature (more like Christ).

The National Geographic *ran an article about the Alaskan Bull Moose. The males of the species battle for dominance during the fall breeding season, literally going head-to-head with antlers crunching together as they collide. Often the antlers, their only weapon, are broken, which ensures defeat.*

The heftiest moose, with the largest and strongest antlers, triumphs. Therefore, the battle fought in the fall is really won during the summer, when the moose eat continually. The one that consumes the best diet for growing antlers and gaining weight will be the heavyweight in the fight. Those that eat inadequately sport weaker antlers and less bulk.[14]

Note

Remind the members of your study group of the basic rules for interpretation of a Scripture passage. These questions must be answered in the mind of the reader:

- **Who** is speaking?
- **To whom** are they speaking?
- **What** is the topic of the conversation?

Group Activity

Ask the study group to help you with a list of things that people spend time and money on in an effort to fill the void (to remove the discontentment and dissatisfaction they are experiencing).

Here are some ideas to start the list:

• Entertainment

• Drugs

• Religion

• Sin

Dedication in being a strong, loyal representative of Christ is best developed before it is needed. What we do now, determines how we will do in spiritual battles later on. We will be victorious or we will fail, depending on our diet. Of course the best diet is to *"abide in His Word."*

Our understanding, accepting, and living the truth is the basis for on-going fellowship with Christ. Let's look at the idea of fellowship with God. The Bible says:

> *"God is faithful, through whom you were called into fellowship with His Son Jesus Christ, our Lord."*
>
> I Corinthians 1:9 NASV

God actually desires to have fellowship (loyal friendship) with us.

Can you believe that?! What an awesome deal: that our Creator and Savior would also want to be our close friend!

Why Should We Have Fellowship With God?

We need fellowship with God. God is a relational Person, and we are created in His image. We have a void within our spirit that only God can fill. People, who are not aware of this, spend a lot of time and money trying to fill the void with the wrong things, and they are never fulfilled. There will always be something else for which they will continue to pursue, because they are trying to fill a legitimate longing in the wrong way. They will always experience the discontentment and dissatisfaction that goes with not having that close mutual friendship with Christ.

In September of 1857, the USS Central American encountered a hurricane while en route from the California gold mines to New York City. The ship and its treasure were discovered a couple of years ago, off the coast of South Carolina. The ship had started out with 500 passengers and a cargo of three tons of gold nuggets, assay bars, and coins worth an estimated one billion dollars. For three days the passengers and crew bailed water, hoping to save the ship, but they were unsuccessful. Of the 500 people on board, 425 drowned.

Survivors told of passengers jumping overboard fatally weighed down with gold. Their desire for gold kept them from survival.[15]

Often, what we think will satisfy our needs will only weigh us down. Paul tells us about people who:

> *"are not serving our Lord Christ, but their own appetites."*
>
> Romans 16:18 NIV

The term **"appetites"** is also translated **"innermost longings."**[16] This is referring to our deep desires to be fulfilled. Whatever we long for most, controls our life. The Bible describes this person as one:

> *"whose end is destruction, whose God is their appetites (innermost longings)..."*
>
> Philippians 3:19 NASV

Either we are pursuing close friendship with Christ, because we realize that only He satisfies, or we are moving towards the wrong ways to fill the void deep within our being. Christ is the only One who offers to fill that void perfectly. All alternatives, even the greatest efforts of man, fall short.

> *In the town hall in Copenhagen stands the world's most complicated clock. It took forty years to build at a cost of more than a million dollars. The clock has ten faces, fifteen thousand parts, and is accurate to two-fifths of a second every three hundred years. The clock computes the time of day, the days of the week, the months and years, and the movements of the planets for twenty-five hundred years. Some parts of that clock will not move until twenty-five centuries have passed.*
>
> *What is intriguing about the clock is that it is not accurate. It loses two-fifths of a second every three hundred years. Like all clocks, that timepiece in Copenhagen must be regulated by a more precise clock, the universe itself. That mighty astronomical clock with its billions of moving parts, from atoms to stars, rolls on century after century with movements so reliable that all time on earth can be measured against it.*[17]

People will disappoint you like a watch that loses time. No mere human being is perfect. But Jesus is altogether different. He is the only perfectly reliable Friend in the universe.

Note

The idea of **"fellowship"** can be a hard one to grasp. In the material of this chapter, the terms *"close friendship"* and *"loyalty"* are used interchangeably with *"fellowship"* because they convey the idea of someone who offers confidentiality and trust.

The goal is to convey the idea that Christ is the perfect *"best friend."*

Note

Explain that it is not wrong to have longings for love, significance, security, etc. God created us to have such longings.

The problem is that we often try to fulfill legitimate longings in illegitimate ways. Making wrong choices and using wrong strategies, about how life really works, is where we go wrong.

This is why we need the wisdom from God's Word to let us know how we are put together, and how we need to satisfy our longings in a moral, Biblical way.

Now understand that friendships with family and friends are extremely important. We are certainly created for those relationships, and they meet needs that are specifically designed by our Creator. However, if we are trying to substitute a friendship with Christ by building our life around human friendships only, it won't work. There's something else that we need to understand.

Fellowship Must Be A Free Choice
(By Both People)

In order for God to have the kind of friendship with you and me, that He really wants, He had to give us the freedom to choose. If we did not have a choice, the loyal friendship would not be real. We would be like robots. For true fellowship, both parties have to be free to choose to enter that relationship. Otherwise, the whole thing would be artificial.[18]

As you well know, our free choice has brought much pain and suffering into this world. But that is how much value God puts on authentic fellowship with us. We value the authentic friendship of our children, spouse, parents, and neighbors, who choose to be our friends. Jesus believes that it is so important for fellowship to be voluntary, that He has given us the freedom to choose it.

Jesus made the offer of fellowship with Himself to the Laodicean Christians in Revelation 3:20 NASV.

> *"Behold, I stand at the door and knock. If anyone hears My voice and opens the door, I will come in to him and dine with him, and he with Me."*

The Lord Jesus Christ is speaking to Christians in the church at Laodicea. Although this invitation has often been used as an offer of salvation, it is actually an offer to share a meal together—which is an ancient Middle Eastern way of offering fellowship.[19]

The use of **"anyone"** means the offer is individualized. Fellowship with Christ is a personal and individual experience.

But how would a Christian "open the door" to fellowship with Christ?

Jesus had taught His disciples the answer to this question, and John recorded that information in his Gospel.

> *"If anyone loves Me, he will keep My word; and My Father will love him, and We will come to him and make our home with him."*

> John 14:23 NIV

So, the way to open the door to fellowship with Jesus Christ is to <u>love Him</u> (this refers to being loyal) and <u>obey His Word</u>. Although Christ indwells the believer the moment he puts his trust in Christ, Paul prayed for the believers at Ephesus *"that Christ may dwell in your hearts by faith…"* (Ephesians 3:14, 16-17). He prayed for this experience for his fellow believers, so there is a fellowship of Christ abiding in our lives that is <u>not</u> a part of our being saved. Fellowship happens as we become obedient to His Word.

This special offer of fellowship with God puts us (believers) in a position to respond. How we choose is up to us. We are not programmed machines. We are flesh and blood human beings with a real choice.[20]

Discipleship Is Lordship

The process of making disciples, as the fulfillment of the Great Commission includes:

> *"teaching them to obey everything I have commanded you."*

> Matthew 28:20 NIV

Obedience to commands is placing ourselves under the Lordship of Jesus Christ, who gave the commission.

As we honor this command by our obedience, we become a participant in His fellowship. In this way, we learn more about Christ and our heavenly Father:

When I survey the wondrous cross, on which the Prince of glory died. My richest gain I count but loss, and pour contempt on all my pride.

Were the whole realm of nature mine, that were a present far too small; Love so amazing, so divine, demands my soul, my life, my all.

Isaac Watts

We were created for friendship and discipleship with Christ Jesus our Savior

"He who has My commandments and keeps them, It is he who loves Me. And he who loves Me shall be loved by My Father, and I will love him and disclose Myself to him."

John 14:21 NASV

The kind of **"love"** that Jesus is speaking of here is not the kind that necessarily involves feeling. Rather, it is a decision—a type of loyalty. So, concerning this information, we can rightly say that fellowship with Christ involves His Lordship over our lives.

Fellowship Is Lordship

We have previously said that the way to open the door to fellowship with our Lord is to love Him and obey His word. That makes the Lordship of Christ a requirement for fellowship. He wants us to eventually become like Him. This obedience produces a great friendship with our Savior.

We were created for friendship and discipleship with Christ Jesus our Savior. We are different from those who are not in His family. The following story might help us relate.

A certain man, who collected and experimented with birds, caught a young eagle one day in the woods. He brought it home and put it among the chickens and ducks and turkeys, and gave it chickens' grain to eat, even though it was an eagle, a different kind of bird.

Several years later, a naturalist came to see him and while passing through his barnyard, said: "That bird is an eagle not a chicken."

"Yes," said the owner, "But I have trained it to be a chicken. It is no longer an eagle, it is a chicken, even though it measures 15 feet from tip to tip of its wings."

"No," said the naturalist, "It is an eagle still; it has the heart of an eagle, and I can make it soar high up to the heavens."

"No," the owner said. "It is a chicken, and it will never fly."

They agreed to a test. The naturalist picked up the eagle, held it up and said with great intensity: "You are an eagle, and you belong to the sky—not to this earth; stretch your wings and fly!"

The eagle turned this way and that, and then looking down, saw the chickens eating their grain and down he jumped.

The owner said, "I told you it was a chicken."

"No," replied the naturalist. "It is an eagle. Give it another chance tomorrow."

So the next day he took the bird to the top of the house. "You are an eagle! Stretch out your wings and fly," he commanded. But again the eagle, seeing the chickens feeding, jumped down and fed with them.

"I told you it was a chicken," the convinced owner re-stated.

"No," asserted the naturalist. "It is an eagle, and it has the heart of an eagle; only give it one more chance, and I will make it fly tomorrow."

The next morning, he rose early and took the eagle outside the community and away from the houses, to the foot of a high mountain. The sun was just rising, gilding the top of the mountains with gold, and every crag was glistening in the joy of the beautiful morning. He picked up the eagle and said to it: "You are an eagle. You belong to the sky and not to the earth. Stretch out your wings and fly." The eagle looked around and trembled as if new life were coming to it. It looked straight at the sun. Suddenly it stretched out its wings, and with the screech of an eagle, it mounted higher and higher and never returned. It was an eagle, though it had been kept and treated as a chicken.[10]

Devoted Followers

September 11, 2001 is etched into history as a day when the whole world was changed. Perspectives on life were affected and the economy of our country recoiled from the attack. New terminology like "Ground zero" is now a commonly used phrase.

It's hard to believe that only ten men were needed to bring about such enormous changes and terrible devastation. How could so few do so much?

Thankfully, evil does not have a monopoly on change. Scripture reminds us of that very truth— *"greater is He who is in you than he who is in the world"* (I John 4:4).

We have now seen what Satan can do through a small band of committed terrorists. Now we need to see what God can do through an army of His devoted followers who will *"Abide in Him."*[9]

Note

A good study group discussion could be centered on the wisdom to compare the fleeting pleasure of worldly choices to the lasting, life-giving plans and principles of God.

How do we make good judgments in the midst of a world of pressure and wrong information?

Give personal examples of making godly decisions.

Believers have been created in Christ Jesus for a special purpose. Yet, having grown up around unbelievers, we think that we are meant to live the way they do. The truth is, *we are different*. We were created for a special work that Christ has prepared for us to do. We are to experience the strength to accomplish our purpose by abiding in the fellowship of Jesus Christ. Without Him, we can do nothing.

When Jesus speaks of **"abide in Me,"** He is describing one of the responsibilities of a disciple. This phrase describes the kind of close friendship that a disciple must maintain in order to bear fruit. It is the responsibility of the disciple to abide in Christ. When this condition is fulfilled, there is fruitfulness.[11] Whether or not the Christian abides, depends on his obedience to God's commands.[12]

People are going to try to tell you that if you obey God's Word and become His friend, you'll miss out on the fun—the good things in life. If you follow God's moral standards, you'll miss out on the fun of immoral sex. If you spend the proper time with your family, you'll miss out on time with the boys or the happy hour at the bar. If you dedicate your business to do things ethically, you'll miss out on the profits.

Let me remind you that people who try to fill that void in their life with all the wrong things in all the wrong places, are destroying their life with the things that they think are making life work for them. Reminds me of one of Paul Harvey's stories about how the Eskimos kill a wolf. The account is grisly, but it offers some insight about the self-destructive nature of sin. Hang in there with me. I think you'll get the point.

> *First, the Eskimo coats his knife blade* with animal blood and allows it to freeze. Then he adds another layer of blood, and another, until the blade is completely concealed by frozen blood.
>
> Next, the hunter fixes his knife in the ground with the blade up. When a wolf follows his sensitive nose to the source of the scent and discovers the bait, he licks it, tasting the fresh frozen blood. He begins to lick faster, more and more vigorously, lapping the blade until the keen edge is bare. Feverishly now, harder and harder the wolf licks the blade in the arctic night. So great becomes his craving for blood that the wolf does not notice the razor-sharp sting of the naked blade on his own tongue, nor does he recognize the instant at which his insatiable thirst is being

satisfied by his "own" blood. His carnivorous appetite just craves more—until the dawn finds him dead in the snow.[23]

It is a truth that thirsty people longing to fill the void in their life in the wrong way can be consumed by their own lusts.

Most people think this is all there is to life. They are not aware of the abundant life that Christ has to give. We should fully dedicate ourselves to trusting that Christ, in His wisdom, can guide us through life. If we determine to be like Him and do what He says to do, then we can become an awesome influence on those who are giving us the bad advice. They'll see that our life is the one that produces peace and builds relationships. And if we've got our act together, we can have a life-changing impact on that audience.

What would you say if someone were to ask why you are always so...

honest?
moral?
happy?

Answer

First find out what they would say.

A good answer would be:

"I couldn't be that way if it wasn't for the wisdom of the Bible and God's grace to make that a part of my life. He created life, therefore He knows how to live it."

LOYALTY

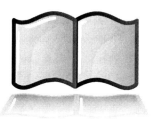

Keeping Our <u>Friendship</u> Strong

Home Improvement *is a sit-com about a man and his partner who give people tips on how to do-it-yourself. They want you to be able to fix what is broken in your home. They tell you how to re-model something that is damaged.*[1]

In our relationship with God, there is room for improvement. He is perfect, but I am not. Then, I have to fix some things about how I am relating to Him. During times when I have become side-tracked into my own strategies for making life work, God will make me aware that the direction I have taken is wrong. (Christians are fallible people, and once-in-a-while, we have to be redirected.) He will make it clear that my thoughts and actions are not compatible with the things that He has commanded.

It is times like this that we must respond in a manner that is appropriate to maintain the magnificent friendship that we, as dedicated believers, have with the Lord. John, the apostle, explains how this friendship works when he says,

> *"If we walk in the light as He is in the light, we have fellowship with one another, and the blood of Jesus Christ, His Son, purifies us from all sin."*

I John 1:7 NIV

It's the words he used about *"walk in the light"* that we must talk about for a moment. John is speaking of people who discover sin in their life while in fellowship with God. You see, while we are walking in fellowship with the Lord, we are in the presence of His light— the light which allows us to recognize the sin,

Leader's Prayer

Pray that, as the members of the study group discover sin in their life, while walking in fellowship with our heavenly Father and with His Son, that they will be open and honest before Him about the sin.

Pray for understanding of this truth.

Leader's Plan

The truth contained in this week's study will require your careful reading and prayerful study in order to clearly understand the principles.

You might try explaining it at home to your spouse or to a friend to see how well the teaching comes across.

This is a special area that Satan would like to keep the members from comprehending.

Hebrews 7:26 says that Jesus Christ is *"Such a high priest...who is holy, blameless, pure, set apart from sinners, exalted above the heavens."*

He is perfect, and therefore, can judge our state of sinfulness with perfect perception.

Note

It might be necessary to explain that our discussion of confession of sin for fellowship has nothing to do with going to Heaven. This series on dedication is all about people who have already settled that issue.

Regarding the issue of Heaven and Hell, we have the assurance of the following promises:

- *"In Him we have...the forgiveness of sins."* Ephesians 1:7

- *"even as God in Christ forgave you."* Ephesians 4:32

- *"And you...He has made alive together with Him, having forgiven you all trespasses."* Colossians 2:13

The theme of the discussion of today's study is the issue of those, who are already saved, maintaining a close fellowship with God by living in a manner that is pleasing to Him.

we become involved in. So, *"walk in the light"* refers to our walking in fellowship with God.

As long as we are walking in the light, we are in a position to be shown our failures.

Verse 5 in chapter 1 of First John says that "God is light and in Him is no darkness at all." This means that God is perfectly free from every kind of moral defect.[2] His perception of sin in our lives is therefore perfect. He is accurate. He doesn't miss-call a thing.

> *Each year the Super Bowl gets more coverage than any other single sporting event. The six hours devoted to pregame and the game itself makes it the network's biggest production of the year. NFL Films, the league's official film and TV company, uses about 150 cinematographers, producers, and technicians for this one game. Their whole entourage includes nearly forty trailers and trucks. They use twenty-eight cameras and shoot about twenty-five miles of film. Yet, with all of this coverage, not everything is filmed. Even though most every angle is covered, some shots will be missed.*[21]

But when we are walking in the light with God, He sees everything perfectly, because He is perfectly holy. He is able to accurately identify self-centeredness, a critical spirit, bitterness, immoral thoughts, unforgiveness, and every thought or action that is not consistent with the character that He wants to develop in us.

So, when He brings some sin to our attention, that puts us in a position to have to deal with a problem that we know has been accurately identified as: (1) sin, (2) our fault, (3) and having no place in our lives. Continued fellowship is based on our willingness to acknowledge the sins that are revealed by His light.

This brings us to the phrase, *"as He is in the light."* This doesn't mean that we are to live in sinless perfection. We are not capable of doing that on this side of Heaven.

Remember that the definition of "fellowship" is actual participation in or sharing in something with another person. Fellowship with God involves sharing the light of His truth and living accordingly. So, *"as He is in the light"* means that we are honest and open in His presence to everything He shows us.[3]

> **When we go through the airport**, *the authorities there put our suitcase and carryon through a certain kind of light. Your baggage must go through their X-ray machine. If you refuse to open your self up to this kind of light, you forfeit your privilege to fly.*[4]

If we refuse to submit to the inspection by God's light, we forfeit the privilege of fellowship. By denying what the light shows, we have ceased to be honest and open with God's evaluation of our condition and fellowship as friends comes to an end. Our effort to avoid His focus on our need for change grieves the Lord. It's evidence that our love for ourselves is greater than our love and trust of our close infinite Friend.

When something about us is exposed as being sinful, our first inclination is to deny it. And if denial is not possible, our next thought is to minimize it. We'll offer excuses, justify and shift the blame. We rethink past events in an effort to prove that we didn't do what we just did, or to prove that what we just did is not as bad as it was.[5] We ignore the moral promptings of God by throwing out arguments and excuses in an attempt to defy our conscious.[7] When our image is on the line, we'll do all kinds of things to protect it.

We feel that somehow we must defend ourselves, otherwise, we'll have to face the shame involved with the truth about who we are. We try to avoid this pain at all cost.

Blinded by our own self-protective excuses, we fail to see that we are actually denying what God has stated to be factual. If we deny what He has revealed about our sins, we have charged God with untruthfulness. We have called Him a liar.

Our friendship with God is much like our human friendships. If we are not honest and above board, but rather choose to deal in falsehood and half-truths, rather than admit our wrongs, we will destroy fellowship with family and friends.

We forget that it is God who is our best friend and that He has our best interest at heart. He loves us and desires only good for us, not bad.

"Walking in the light as He is in the light"
This phrase means that we are open and honest about everything that He reveals to us about sin in our life.[3]

Discussion
Ask the study group to suggest ways that denials and excuses are expressed. What do people say when they are confronted by a friend about something they have done wrong?

Here are several that you can use to keep the activity going:

- *"Well, you do things just as bad."*

- *"You never notice the good things that I do."*

- *"If you just understood what led up to this."*

- *"I was just telling it like it is."*

- *"A person has a right to speak their mind, don't they?"*

- *"If you realized what I really felt like, you'd understand that I was controlling myself."*[8]

Several years ago a newspaper reported this story that happened on the east coast. One evening a woman was driving home when she noticed a huge truck behind her that was driving uncomfortably close. She stepped on the gas to gain some distance from the truck, but when she sped up, the truck did too. The faster she drove, the faster the truck followed behind.

Now scared, she exited the freeway. But the truck stayed with her. The woman then turned up a main street, hoping to lose her pursuer in traffic. But the truck ran a red light and continued the chase.

Reaching the point of panic, the woman whipped her car into a service station and bolted out of her auto screaming for help. The truck driver sprang from his truck and ran toward her car. Yanking the back door open, the driver pulled out a man hidden in the back seat.

The woman was running from the wrong person. From his high vantage point, the truck driver had spotted a would-be rapist in the woman's car. The chase was not his effort to harm her but to save her, even at the cost of his own safety.[28]

Running from God is due to a misunderstanding of His motives and plans. He has a higher vantage point and knows about things that have great potential danger to our lives. Though He wants only to rescue us from the hidden sins that endanger our lives, many of us are running away, fearing what He might do.

God's Warning System is Designed to Protect Our Life.

When God warns us about specific sin in our life, He is actually showing His love and grace to us. As we appreciate that truth and adhere to His timely warnings, we may avoid the danger and disaster that would result from that sin.

In Walter Lord's book, Day of Infamy, *there is given a stirring account of the attack on Pearl Harbor. Not only does it describe the horror of that historic day, but it spells out a tragedy that is equally disconcerting…the length of time it took people to realize they were under attack. Japanese Zeroes were screaming through the air and bombs were exploding everywhere, but most people just thought it was a drill. One seaman had the sentiments of many, "Somebody is going to catch it for putting live bombs on those planes."*

A quicker response to the attack would have prevented much of the destruction.[11]

What a picture of our situation as God's friend, walking with Him through this culture. We are under full-scale attack by the world system and our own sin nature, yet many view it as simply a drill. It is high time for us to hear and respond to the alarms that the Lord is **sounding**!

Lou Little coached football for Columbia University *a number of years ago. One day Lou had a boy try out for the varsity team who wasn't really very good. But Lou noticed that there was something unique about him—while he wasn't nearly good enough to make the team, he had such irrepressible spirit and contagious enthusiasm that Lou thought, "This boy could be a great inspiration on the bench. He'll never be able to play, but I'll leave him on the team to encourage the others."*

As the season went on, Lou began to develop a tremendous admiration for this boy. One of the things that especially impressed him was the manner with which the boy obviously cared for his father. Whenever the father would come for a visit to the campus the boy and his father would always be seen walking together. They could always be seen on Sunday going to and from the university chapel. It was obvious that theirs was a deep and mutually shared Christian faith.

Then, one day, a telephone call came to Coach Little. He was informed that the boy's father had just died—would he be the one to tell the boy? With a heavy heart, Lou informed the boy of his father's death, and he immediately left to go home for the funeral. A few days later the boy returned to the campus, only two days before the biggest game of the season. Lou went to him and said, "Is there anything I can do for you, anything at

Discussion

Some members of the study group might think that God is out to keep us from having fun, when He reveals to us the truth about our sins, through the light of His Word. Actually, He is a caring Father, who wants to ensure our success in this life. God is like a wise coach, who is determined to improve our game.

So, while we once thought of God as One who wants to rob us of the good times, now, through a better understanding of His character and love, we can view Him as being for us, rather than being against us.

Illustration

Many electronic fire alarms have an internal switch triggered by a beam of light. As long as light is received unbroken by the photo-sensitive receiver, the detector is quiet. But if smoke or moisture or an insect obstructs the beam for even a split second, the alarm sounds.[12]

Our conscience resembles such an alarm. When sin obstructs our connection with the light of God's Spirit, the conscience signals us that there's life-threatening danger.

Memory Verse

I John 1:9

Scripture

This Scripture could be referenced in their Bibles in the margin beside I John 1:7.

"Surely You desire truth in the inward parts…Create in me a pure heart, O God, and renew a steadfast spirit within me." Psalm 51:6,10

"Confess"

Confess means "to agree or admit" (in judicial language "make a confession"),[9]

"At the heart of it, confession involves taking appropriate responsibility for what we have done."[10]

all?" And to the coach's astonishment the boy said, *"Let me start the game on Saturday!"* Lou was taken back. He thought, *"I can't let him start—he's not good enough."* But he remembered his promise to help and said, *"Alright—you can start the game,"* and he thought to himself, *"I'll leave him in for a few plays and then take him out."*

The day of the big game arrived. To everyone's surprise the coach started this boy who had never played in a game all season. But imagine even the coach's surprise when, on the very first play from scrimmage, that boy was the one who single-handedly made a tackle that threw the opposing team for a loss. The boy went on to play inspired football play after play. In fact, he played so exceptionally that Lou left him in for the entire game; the boy led his team to victory, and he was voted the outstanding player of the game.

When the game was finally over, Lou approached the boy and said, "Son, what got into you today?" And the boy replied, "You remember when my father would visit me here at school and we would spend a lot of time together walking around the campus? You see, my father and I shared a secret that nobody around here knew anything about. You see, my father was blind—and today was the first time he ever saw me play!"[13]

Since our heavenly Father sees every move we make, we are able to *"play above our heads"* in this life. His love and desire for us to be winners should inspire us to make it our best game.

If We Are Walking Openly and Honestly Before God, <u>What's Next</u>?

God showed me my sin. Yes, I see it as sin. What do I do? What happens now? We should **confess** our sin.

> *"If we confess our sins, He is faithful and just to forgive us our sins and purify us from all unrighteousness."*
>
> I John 1:9 NIV

"Confess" means to agree, admit or acknowledge that what God has revealed to us about our sins is true. Keep in mind that at any given time, we may not be conscious that the thing we are doing is wrong. *That* sin is revealed to us. So, rather than denying the sin, we agree with God that it is indeed sin. When we do this, God forgives our sin. He is faithful to do so. We can count on Him.

In this confession, we avoid being judged and therefore disciplined for that sin. It's a chance to erase the slate and get things right this time. I Corinthians 11:31-32 explains this truth very clearly.

> **"But if we judge ourselves, we would not come under judgment. When we are judged by the Lord, we are being disciplined so that we will not be condemned with the world."**
>
> I Corinthians 11:31-32 NIV

In his book, *The Life You've Always Wanted*, John Ortberg tells about the day that he and his wife traded in their old Volkswagen Super Beetle for:

> ...***our first piece of furniture***—*a mauve sofa. It was roughly the shade of Pepto-Bismol, but because it represented to us a substantial investment, we thought "mauve" sounded better.*
>
> *The man at the furniture store warned us not to get it when he found out we had small children. "You don't want a mauve sofa," he advised. "Get something the color of dirt." But we had the naïve optimism of young parenthood. "We know how to handle our children," we said. "Give us the mauve sofa."*
>
> *From that moment on, we all knew clearly the number one rule in the house: "Don't sit on the mauve sofa. Don't touch the mauve sofa. Don't play around the mauve sofa. Don't eat on, breath on, look at, or think about the mauve sofa. Remember the forbidden tree in the Garden of Eden? On every other chair in the house you may freely sit, but upon this sofa, the mauve sofa, you may not sit, for in the day you sit thereupon, you shall surely die."*
>
> *Then came the Fall.*
>
> *One day there appeared on the mauve sofa a stain. A red stain. A red jelly stain.*

Scripture

Proverbs 28:13 is another Scripture that should be referenced with I John 1:9.

"He who covers his sins will not prosper, but whoever confesses and forsakes them will have mercy." Proverbs 28:13

Note

Even though judgment and discipline can be avoided by confession, there are other serious matters that we must face.

- First, we cannot <u>plan</u> a sin, carry it out, confess it, and avoid the discipline. The planning of such a strategy is a sin in itself. It is deciding to do what we know is wrong. Discipline would be the consequence of such a plan.

- James 4:6 says, *"God is opposed to the proud, but gives grace to the humble."*

- Second, there are <u>natural consequences</u> to our sinful actions and reactions that we cannot side step. For example, cutting words, spoken in anger, can cause a hurt that might never be removed.

The class might discuss other natural results of sin that are not possible to change—even though we are forgiven.

Occasionally, I John 1:9 is used as a verse that is meant for the unsaved. This view of the verse does not take into account the audience to whom John is writing.

The message in I John about confession is written to believers.

- *"I do not write to you because you do not know the truth, but because you know it…"* I John 2:21

- *"But the anointing which you have received of Him abides in you…"* I John 2:27

- *"And now dear children continue in Him…"* I John 2:28

- *"Behold, what manner of love the Father has bestowed upon us, that we should be called the sons of God…"* I John 3:1

Note

The incredible truth is that when we honestly acknowledge whatever sins we are aware of, the cleansing that follows covers everything that needs cleansing.

What a friend we have in Jesus!

So my wife, who had chosen the mauve sofa and adored it, lined up our three children in front of it: Laura, age four, and Mallory, two and a half, and Johnny, six months.

"Do you see that, children?" she asked. "That's a stain. A red stain. A red jelly stain. The man at the sofa store says it is not coming out. Not forever. Do you know how long forever is, children? That's how long we're going to stand here until one of you tells me who put the stain on the mauve sofa."

Mallory was the first to break. With trembling lips and tear-filled eyes she said, "Laura did it." Laura passionately denied it. Then there was silence, for the longest time. No one said a word. I knew the children wouldn't, for they had never seen their mother so upset. I knew they wouldn't, because they knew that if they did, they would spend eternity in the time-out chair.

I knew they wouldn't, because I was the one who put the red jelly stain on the mauve sofa, and I knew I wasn't saying anything. I figured I would find a safe place to confess—such as in a book I was going to write, maybe."[14]

Ortberg goes on to say that we have all stained the sofa.[15] I am personally thankful to our loving and forgiving Lord that, unlike the mauve sofa, the stain in our life can be removed.

By agreeing with God, with our own words, that what we've done is sinful, we are less likely to make such a wrong choice again. In confessing, our goal should be to set things right between us and our Lord, not just to avoid painful consequences.

What About the Sins That We <u>Don't</u> Confess?

You might be troubled by the idea that you have failed to confess all of your sins. After all, who can possibly know <u>all</u> of their sins? So, what about the sins of which we are unaware? Since we cannot confess what we do not know, God says that if we confess the sins we do know, He will take care of the rest.

When we acknowledge what we know to be wrong, the other sins in our life, that have not been revealed to us, are cleansed away.[16] This is what John means by the phrase: *"and to cleanse us from all unrighteousness."* So, when we are honest about the sins that we do know, whatever other sins that may be in our life are totally cleansed away. The *"all unrighteousness"* is a term broad enough to cover every kind of wickedness, injustice, wrongdoing, or deception.[17]

This kind of faithfulness by our Father in Heaven can only encourage us to respond truthfully as He reveals our need for change in character.

How **Often** Should We Confess Our Sins?

We should confess a sin as soon as we are aware that what we are doing is wrong. Otherwise, we will no longer be walking in the fellowship of Christ. This affects our communication with God. Psalm 66:18 KJV warns us that:

> *"If I regard iniquity in my heart, the LORD will not hear."*

Jesus taught His disciples to pray daily, and in His example of how to pray, He said:

> *"...Give us this day our <u>daily</u> bread and <u>forgive us our debts</u>..."*
>
> Matthew 6:11-12a KJV

The key is to admit, confess, and ask God immediately to forgive our sins as we are made aware of them. Continuing in sin can cause us to miss out on present effectiveness for Christ. We will also lose future rewards.

> *In the 1994 New York Marathon, German Silva, born in a tiny, impoverished village in rural Mexico, was 700 yards from victory. He had trained for 26 years. His dream was for something better for his mother, his people and his village. Back home there was no sports coverage on T. V. There wasn't even any electricity, so his mother waited anxiously for word of his success.*
>
> *Silva had now run almost 26 miles. Trailing close behind was his friend and frequent training partner, Benjamine Paredes. Together, they had assumed control of the race at the 23-mile mark. Stride for stride, they matched each other through Central Park.*

Security

The sins of a believer do not result in a loss of eternal salvation. They do, however, interrupt our personal friendship with God our heavenly Father. Forgiveness restores that friendship.

Note

The purpose for admitting and confessing our sins is not just to make life work out the way we wish. That should not become the primary goal of our Christian life.

Rather, our goal must be to continue to experience nearness to God. Fellowship with Him is "the best that heaven has to offer."[23]

There's nothing wrong with wanting life to run more smoothly. But we should not "seek the better life of God's blessings over the better hope of God's presence."[24]

Ask the students to turn with you to Matthew 18:21-35. Here is an even more in-depth description of how the Lord feels about our showing mercy through forgiving our fellow man.

As you can see, this parable is part of the answer to a question from Peter. Verse 22 is the incredible statement from Jesus about forgiveness:

"I tell you, not seven times, but seventy–seven times."

Read the entire narrative, v.21-35 together, and allow time for comments by the students.

Some key points of discussion might be:

• *"The servant's master took pity on him and cancelled the debt."* v.27

• *"You wicked servant"* v.32

• *"In anger his master turned him over to the jailers"* v.34

The "ten thousand talents" in v. 24 had a value of $10,000,000 in silver content, but worth much more in buying power.[20]

Memory Verse
Matthew 6:14-15

The most celebrated New York Marathon in history was about to see the most exciting conclusion. Silva remained confident. He knew that, if it came down to a sprint, he was the fastest runner.

Just ahead of him, the camera car set the pace as the crew aboard captured the dramatic climax of the race. Physically and mentally exhausted, Silva focused on the back of the vehicle and steadily increased his lead.

With only hundreds of yards to go, the camera car made a right turn, leaving Central Park. Silva followed close behind. The cheering crowd suddenly turned their celebration into distress. Silva sensed that something was wrong. A policeman pointed back toward Central Park. Silva realized that he was off course.

Now his friend had a 50-yard lead. Silva had never outrun Peredes enough to make up for such a deficit. Nevertheless, he returned to the course and began a feverish sprint toward the finish line.

Less than 2/10 of a mile to go, Silva caught up with Peredes. He won by two seconds, the smallest lead in the marathon's history, and received $150,000.[18]

Silva narrowly escaped the sport's disaster of a lifetime![19] In a few critical seconds, all his talent and years of training had taken a turn in the wrong direction. With the help of a distressed crowd and a policeman's direction, he recognized his error and got quickly back on course.

There's no doubt that God wants us to win. He points the way back to the course. Daily—yes even instantly, as we are made aware of our direction, we are to confess.

Oh, Yes, There's One Other Thing!

If we want the Lord to forgive us (and we do), we must also forgive those who have sinned against us. A few moments ago we were talking about the Lord's prayer example. Let's look at it once more:

"and forgive us our sins, just as we have forgiven those who have sinned against us..."

Matthew 6:12 NLT

Well there it is, plain as day. Forgiving others is critical for our being forgiven. This vital information, which keeps us on course, is given in a bit more detail in verse 14 and 15 of the same chapter.

"If you forgive those who sin against you, your heavenly Father will forgive you. But if you refuse to forgive others, your Father will not forgive your sins."

Matthew 6:14-15 NLT

The issue of forgiveness is so important that it deserved an extra comment after the Lord had made forgiveness a part of His model prayer. Believe me, this is a real vital coaching point for our walking in the light as He is in the light! When we are in His fellowship, forgiving others is a doable task.

Dedicating ourselves to become like Christ does not mean that we will become instantly mature. Rather, we grow more like Him as we learn more about what we need to change. As Christ teaches us about our bad thoughts, words, and actions, and we respond truthfully, our maturity keeps on increasing.

How thankful we should be for the opportunity to change direction.

God's Word About Our Sin is the Final Authority

The captain of a battle ship looked into the dark night and saw faint lights in the distance. Immediately he told his signalman to send a message: "Alter your course 10 degrees south."

*Promptly a return message was received: "Alter **your** course 10 degrees north."*

The captain was angered; his command had been ignored. So he sent a second message: "Alter your course 10 degrees south— I am the captain!"

Note

Maturity is a process, not an event. It requires "**practice**" to be able to discern between good and evil.

"But solid food is for the mature, who because of practice, have their senses trained to discern good and evil." Hebrews 5:14

Ask the students to turn to this verse in their Bibles and write the reference I John 1:9 in the margin.

Discussion

Members of the study group might share some personal experience when they received great benefit from the light of God's Word. Perhaps a friend shared some Scripture that exposed the danger of the path they were on.

They might also wish to express their thoughts about making one of the goals of their Christian life to walk in fellowship with Christ, as His close friend.

The process of maturity is also seen in Eph. 4:22-24.

"You were taught, with regard to your former way of life, to put off your old self, which is being corrupted by its deceitful desires, and that you be renewed in the attitude of your mind, and to put on the new self, created to be like God in true righteousness and holiness."

The "old self" refers to our old nature.

Illustration

For eight years, Sally had been the Romero family pet. When they got her, she was only one foot long. But Sally grew until eventually she reached eleven and one-half feet and weighed 80 pounds.

Then on July 20, 1993, Sally, a Burmese python, turned on 15-year-old Derek, strangling the teenager until he died of suffocation. Associated Press Online (7/22/93) quoted the police as saying that the snake was "quite aggressive, hissing, and reacting" when they arrived to investigate.[26]

Although sin seems harmless at first, it will grow and it will eventually lead to death, if we tolerate it.

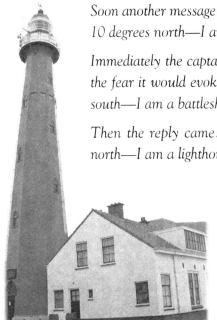

Soon another message was received: "Alter your course 10 degrees north—I am seaman third class."

Immediately the captain sent a third message, knowing the fear it would evoke: "Alter your course 10 degrees south—I am a battleship."

Then the reply came: "Alter your course 10 degrees north—I am a lighthouse."[21]

When God shines His light on our life and reveals needed change, we have our own ideas about the direction of our ship. His signals run contrary to our plans. But He happens to be the Light of the World, and we ignore Him at our own peril. The purpose of a light house is to protect ships. Its light keeps them from being destroyed by large jagged rocks, hidden beneath the surface of the water. There is danger that doesn't meet the eye.

We can be so easily fooled by the deceptiveness of sin. That is why we need the light of God's word to help us comprehend the danger involved. It can destroy our lives.

A young brave struggled with all of his strength to climb the highest mountain peak where his reward would be the eagle feather. He extended all of his strength and tested his will to the max to stand there with hands raised in victory, celebrating his achievement.

At his feet, a snake looked up at the young brave and said, "Please help me. I am cold up here. Take me to the bottom of the mountain."

The young brave replied, "No way! I'm not picking you up. You would bite and kill me."

"No," said the snake, denying the obvious. "I won't bite you. I promise."

"Yes, you will," protested the young brave.

The snake replied, "All I want is to get off the mountain. Take me down where it is warm, and I won't hurt you."

Stooping down, the young brave picked up the snake and put it within his coat to take him down the mountain. At the base of the mountain, he reached in to retrieve the snake only to experience a sharp pain in his hand where the fangs penetrated into his bloodstream. The hot poison moved its way through his veins to his heart, and the young brave felt instantly weak. His vision grew darker and darker, and he realized death was imminent.

He muttered to the snake, "You promised not to hurt me. Why did you bite me? You promised me."

And the snake replied cynically, "You knew what I was when you picked me up."[29]

At a time when we are just beginning to live, the hidden deadliness of sin will destroy our life with all of our dreams, if we pick it up.

The disguised consequences of sin can be avoided by taking God's evaluation of our sin and maintaining our commitment to stay away from, avoid, and flee from it.

To avoid disaster, we simply do what God says about sin in order to be forgiven and cleansed.

In 1818, Ignaz Phillip Semmelweis was born into a world of dying women. The finest hospitals lost one out of six young mothers to the scourge of "childbed fever."

A doctor's daily routine began in the dissecting room where he performed autopsies. From there he made his way to the hospital to examine expectant mothers without ever pausing to wash his hands. Dr. Semmelweis was the first man in history to associate such examinations with the resultant infection and death. His own practice was to wash with a chlorine solution, and after eleven years and the delivery of 8,537 babies, he lost only 184 mothers—about one in fifty.

He was faithful to do needed research. Once he argued, "puerperal fever is caused by decomposed material conveyed to a wound...I have shown how it can be prevented, I have proved

Illustration

There is a temptation to soften and dilute warnings in hopes of not sounding too harsh or alarming. The danger of such soft-peddling can be seen in the tobacco industry. In a test of nearly 2,500 children in the U.S. and Canada, 83% could remember the warning on Canadian cigarettes, but only 6% were able to recall what was printed on U.S. cigarette packs. The reason is simple. In Canada, the warning is clear and direct. On the front of the package in bold letters you read these words, "**Smoking can kill you.**"

Softening a deadly message doesn't reduce the danger.

Edward DeHart died of lung cancer on September 24, 1997. In 1962, DeHart developed the warning labels printed on cigarette packs sold in the United States. The warning that he created wasn't convincing enough to even make *him* stop smoking.

Houston Chronicle, 9/29/79, p.10

Illustration

*Autobiography in Five
Short Chapters*

—Portia Nelson

Chapter 1 — I walk down the street. There is a deep hole in the sidewalk. I fall in. I am lost...I am helpless. It isn't my fault. It takes forever to find a way out.

Chapter 2 — I walk down the same street. There is a deep hole in the sidewalk. I pretend I don't see it. I fall in again. I can't believe I am in the same place, but it isn't my fault. It still takes a long time to get out.

Chapter 3 — I walk down the same street: There is a deep hole in the sidewalk. I see it is there. I still fall in...It's a habit. My eyes are open. I know where I am. It is my fault. I get out immediately.

Chapter 4 — I walk down the same street. There is a deep hole in the sidewalk. I walk around it.

Chapter 5 — I walk down another street.[27]

Well, if God is going to forgive my sin as soon as I confess it, why not go ahead and sin, because He's going to forgive it anyway?

all that I have said. But while we talk, talk, talk, gentlemen, women are dying. I am not asking anything world shaking. I am asking you only to wash...For God's sake, wash your hands." But virtually no one believed him. Doctors and midwives had been delivering babies for thousands of years without washing, and no outspoken Hungarian was going to change them now! Semmelweis died insane at the age of 47, his wash basins discarded, his colleagues laughing in his face, and the suffering of a thousand women ringing in his ears.[22]

A believer, who refuses to be cleansed from all unrighteousness, can "infect" the life of others through bad influence. When God asks us to follow His simple principle about confession of sins, He's not asking "*anything world shaking.*" He is simply asking us to be cleansed.

In the book of James, we read this formula:

> **"but each one is tempted, when, by his own evil desire, he is dragged away and enticed. Then, after desire has conceived, it gives birth to sin; and sin when it is full-grown, gives birth to death."**
>
> James 1:14-15 NIV

The Bible teaches that physical death can be a consequence of not being cleansed from our sin, just as it can be a consequence of poor medical practices.

Some Will Not Take Sin <u>Seriously</u>

Because of our Lord's provision of forgiveness when we confess our sins, some believers take sin lightly and therefore do not put forth any real effort to keep *from* sinning. John, the apostle, addresses this possibility of abusing God's grace. He lets us know that sin is a serious issue between God and believers.

> **"My dear children, these things I write unto you <u>so that you may not sin</u>. But if anybody does sin, we have an Advocate with the Father—Jesus Christ the Righteous."**
>
> I John 2:1 NIV

The fact is that we *should*, by God's word and His grace, resist sin. It is also true that we will not achieve perfection. So if, and when we sin, our Lord Jesus Christ speaks on our behalf to the Father. Jesus is praying! He is our "advocate." What does it mean to be an advocate? What is our Lord Jesus actually doing for us, when we make sinful choices?

Jesus is our Great High Priest. Being our advocate with the Father means that He is *praying* for us. He wants us to succeed in a life of growth and maturity, as we experience successes and failures.

Jesus has left us with a good illustration of how He prays for a believer in times of failure. In Luke 22:31-33 we have been given an example of some things for which Jesus prayed, knowing that very soon, Peter would deny that he even knew Him.

> *"Simon, Simon, behold, Satan has asked to sift you like wheat. But I have prayed for you, Simon, that your faith may not fail. And when you have turned back, strengthen your brothers."*
>
> Luke 22:31-33 NIV

Zane Hodges, in his commentary on *The Epistles of John*,[26] lists three areas of Peter's life that Jesus addressed in His prayer:

(1) Jesus prayed for the strengthening of Peter's faith during the time of testing—*"that your faith may not fail."*

(2) He prayed for Peter's spiritual recovery and restoration to fellowship—*"when you have turned back."*

(3) Jesus also prayed for Peter's future usefulness in ministry—*"strengthen your brothers."*

Jesus Christ, our faithful High Priest, prays for our strengthened faith, spiritual recovery, and future usefulness. It is our responsibility to avoid sin, but in a time of failure to do so, we are not abandoned. Jesus Christ is a merciful and faithful high priest:

> *"Because He Himself suffered when He was tempted, He is able to help those who are being tempted."*
>
> Hebrews 2:18 NIV

Note

Paul was very clear on the issue of avoiding sin:

"Shall we sin that grace may abound? God forbid!"
Romans 6:1

"Advocate"
"One who appears on another's behalf, mediator, intercessor, helper"[25]

Note

In I John 2:1, Jesus is not pleading, as a lawyer, for the Father to keep us saved. Romans 8:33 says:

"Who will bring a charge against God's elect? God is the One who justifies."

No charge can be laid against us regarding justification. Christ's death paid for all human sin for everyone <u>for all time</u>.

"but He, having offered one sacrifice for sins, for all time, sat down at the right hand of the Father."
Hebrews 10:12

Plan Ahead

You could ask a local pastor to come to your study group and lead them in participating together in communion as they remember the great love that was shown in Christ's death for us.

"And while they were eating, Jesus took some bread, and after a blessing, He broke it and gave it to the disciples, and said, 'Take, eat; this is My body.' And when He had taken a cup and given thanks, He gave it to them, saying, 'Drink from it, all of you; for this is My blood of the covenant, which is poured out for many for forgiveness of sins.'"

Matthew 26:26-28

There is a special need for us to retain in our memory the great sacrifice that our Lord made in our place. Jesus gave instructions to His eleven disciples and later on to Paul about passing on a valuable tradition to the church. It is called "communion." It's something that believers participate in together.

COMMUNION

A special way to remember what Jesus has done for us as our Savior and High Priest is to participate together in the ordinance of communion in our local church.

Communion is the same word that we translate "fellowship." It means to participate or share in something together. One activity that we participate in or share with Christ is "walking in the light." We do this when we agree together about the changes that we need to make in our character and conduct, as His close friends.

The participation involved in a communion service in our local church, has to do with showing forth the Lord's death, until He returns. As a local church congregation, we are participating together as a witness to the fact that Jesus died in our place as a substitute. We are stating that we have personally participated in the benefits of the death of Jesus Christ, by trusting Him as our only way to Heaven. Paul explains to the Corinthians:

"For I received from the Lord what I also passed on to you: The Lord Jesus, on the night He was betrayed, took bread, and when He had given thanks, He broke it and said, 'This is My body, which is for you; do this in remembrance of Me.' In the same way, after supper He took the cup, saying, 'This cup is the new covenant in My blood; do this, whenever you drink it, in remembrance of Me.' For whenever you eat this bread

and drink this cup, you proclaim the Lord's death until He comes."

I Corinthians 11:23-26

By joint-participation in this eating of the bread and drinking of the cup, we are thinking about (reminiscing about) our greatest Friend, the One who died in our place. We are saying together (proclaiming publicly) the fact and significance of the death of Christ: that He died as our *substitute*.

This is something that we are doing for Christ our Lord. He said, **"Do this in remembrance of Me."** Someone said that this is the only request that Jesus made for Himself. We participate together in memory of Christ **"until He comes."**

What About Receiving Communion "Unworthily"?

This is not referring to a lack of personal merit. No one deserves it! The term **"unworthily"** is an *adverb*, so it should be **"in an unworthy manner."** Which would mean to participate without a respect for what it represents. It would be like taking communion in a careless, thoughtless manner.[30]

Note

The word *"for"* in verse 24 means "on behalf of."

This points to the death of Christ as being a substitute for our own death. He was there in our place.

The word *"broken"* is in some translations. However, it is printed in italics, because it does not appear in the manuscripts.

CHARACTER PART I

What Kind of <u>People</u> are We Becoming?

Character is the courage to do what God defines as right, regardless of the cost.[1] It is a moral strength that is acquired and increased as we continue to allow our minds to be transformed by the truth of the Scriptures. It doesn't happen over night. Character development is a process.

Charlie Waters, former strong safety for the Dallas Cowboys, tells a story about Frank Howard who was Charlie's college coach.

> **When Frank Howard was head coach** at Clemson University, he went out to practice one Monday before a big game with his 1st and 3rd string QBs out with injuries. That left him with his 2nd, 4th, and 5th string QBs to play the coming Saturday.
>
> In the first five minutes of practice, his (now) 1st string QB (who had been the 2nd stringer) hurt his knee. That elevated the 4th stringer to the 1st string and put the 5th stringer on the 2nd team.
>
> About 10 minutes later, that QB hurt his knee. Now, the 5th stringer was next in line for 1st team. Coach Howard blew the whistle and gathered all the remaining players around him. He took the one remaining QB, put his arm around him and said in his gruff voice, "Son, do you believe in magic?" The QB said in a half-hearted way, "Well, sorta." Coach Howard looked at him, pointed his fingers at him like a magician, and said, "Poof! You are now a first string quarter back."[2]

We expect the Christian life to work in the same manner—"Poof! You have perfect Christian character." But, as you know, that 5th string QB had

"Character"
The courage to do what God defines as right, regardless of the cost.[2]

Leader's Prayer
Pray that it will make sense to each person to develop godly character qualities. Pray that the value of becoming transformed will be clearly evident to them and that their desire to become like Christ will affect their choices in daily living.

Leader's Plan
Since it is true that when we are saved, we are not born again with a perfect Godly character, the group needs to know that the character building process starts after we are saved and continues throughout our lifetime.

Prepare to share some learning experiences of your own.

"...train yourself to be godly."

I Timothy 4:7

A Monumental Work

The work that occurred from 1927 to 1941 yielded four 60-foot-tall presidential portraits that reflect the stubborn determination of the sculptor and the small cadre of hardworking miners he guided in carving a mountain into one of the wonders of the modern world.[11]

This great work of art took fourteen years to accomplish. Like our character, the work of art performed on the "four faces of freedom" on this mountain was not achieved in a short amount of time. Character is not a course you can take on the internet. It takes time, real life experience and right choices as God's word is allowed to transform new believers into the people that He wants us to become.

been involved in a training process during those months and years prior to the pronouncement by Frank Howard. He was already prepared and waiting in the wings until his time came to play the leading role.

Now the question is: "How is character development accomplished?"

The character development process is explained by Peter:

> **"...but grow in the grace and knowledge of our Lord and Savior Jesus Christ..."**
>
> II Peter 3:18

When Bruce Bugbee wrote the book, *What You Do Best*, he explained the normal process that we go through when we put a large puzzle together:

> *1st get all the colored sides facing up—2nd, look for the straight edges that form the sides of the puzzle, keeping an eye out for the four corner pieces (they have two straight edges)—3rd, set the box lid up, so you can see what the finished product looks like—4th, put the border together—then put the remaining pieces inside.*

He then said that pouring the pieces out on the table will not produce an accurate picture. The process of putting the pieces together leads to a finished picture.[5]

All the elements for Christian character are in the Bible. Those elements are important pieces of a formula for transforming us to be more like Christ. You are aware of many of the elements that constitute that kind of person, but I want to put some key pieces together so you will know how to accomplish this task.

The formula is: **Train <u>Well</u> and Try <u>Hard</u>.**

Train well (Practice) refers to a scheduled training procedure and timetable. It would involve the consistent practice of skills and techniques we've learned in the Bible. Try hard (Performance) involves dedicated performance in an all-out effort to put the skills that we've practiced into real life performance. Dedication involves practice as well as performance. Let's look at the training part first.

Train <u>Well</u>

> *"Everyone who competes in the games goes into <u>strict training</u>. They do it to get a crown that will not last; but we do it to get a crown that will last forever."*

> I Corinthians 9:25

Training must come first, but training begins with good coaching. This involves learning the truth about the skill that we want to develop. We need accurate instruction in the techniques and fundamentals.

There's an old principle that says, "Practice makes perfect." This principle is only partially true. Actually, practice makes permanent. So it is

---

Special Note

(Concerning the Downloadable Quiz)

In the material for this week, there are fifteen (15) truths from Scripture. Each of these truths counteracts a specific lie that destroys godly character.

As a summary of each truth and lie, there is a box that contains the **basics** for character training development. These basics are the primary focus for the Quiz for this chapter.

Note

Notice that **training** *must begin first.* Point out to the study group that we do not receive all the training before we begin the **trying**.

Character building involves **trying** *as you* **train**. It is a learn-and-build-skill-as-you-go process.

Practice Decision-Making

Ask the study group to turn to this verse. Explain that it is God's program that we train to make good decisions by practicing making those decisions constantly.

"But solid food is for the mature, who by constant use have **trained** *themselves to distinguish good from evil."* Hebrews 5:14

Class Activity

Ask the class to help you with a list of things you would have to practice in order to play basketball (things you'd do in a game).

Here is a list. See if they can get them all: *free throws, passing the ball, dribbling, rebounding, running, and shooting from various places on the court.*

You might ask the same question about the fundamentals that you would practice in playing in a piano recital or to play in a school band in the Christmas parade.

Additional Scripture

Titus 2:12-13 contains specific instructions about what 'training yourself to be godly' means. Ask the students to turn in their Bibles and reference this verse with I Timothy 4:7.

"...to deny ungodliness and worldly desires and to live sensibly, righteously and godly in the present age, looking for the blessed hope and the appearing of the glory of our great God and Savior, Christ Jesus."
Titus 2:12-13

The students could begin to develop a list of Scripture references about the kind of character qualities that we need to be practicing.

This Scripture reference list can be started in their Bible (on a clear page in the front or back) or in the margin of their study guide.

possible that if we train, using the wrong information, we will learn to do something the wrong way.

During the earlier years of our lives, we've picked up some wrong information from this world system about how life works. I believe that these inaccurate ideas, that we have acquired, are lies that Satan would like for us to continue to use in shaping our character in destructive ways. Our first kind of training is to counteract the lies that we have learned, so we can be practicing the right things. The Scriptures tell us to **"train yourself to be godly."** (1 Timothy 4:7) But the lies that we've picked up along the way, are telling us that that kind of training is not practical in this day and time.

Let's see how our beliefs affect our behavior.

> **In the middle of the 1400's,** *people thought the world was flat. That belief produced fear in the hearts of sailors and captains. Because of that fear, they sailed reasonably close to land, so they would not fall off the edge of the flat earth. What they believed about the shape of the world influenced what they feared and therefore how they sailed their ships.*
>
> *Then Christopher Columbus, as tradition goes, discovered a truth one day while eating an apple. As he was taking a bite, a butterfly lit on the apple and began to crawl over the top to the other side. Columbus noticed that as the butterfly walked to the back of the apple, the last part of the butterfly that he saw was the tips of its wings. For Columbus, that was like watching a ship sail out of sight. The last part of the ship that he saw was the top of the sails. He concluded that the earth must be round.*
>
> *He now believed something different about the earth. That changed his fear of falling off the edge, because now he knew there was no "edge." The elimination of his fear changed his attitude about sailing.[6] He changed man's understanding of the world.*

As long as the captains of the ships believed incorrectly, their fears limited their potential of distance and discovery.[6] As long as you and I believe incorrectly about God, relationships, marriage, anger, etc., it will also shape our behavior and our potential.

The ship captains of the 1400's assumed that their information about the shape of the world was a correct evaluation of things. But, they later found that their assumptions were wrong.

Training in <u>Truth</u>
*(Getting The **Facts** Straight)*

Stephen Covey illustrates how our evaluation of things can affect our emotions, our attitudes, and our responses. The following is his personal experience one morning on a New York subway.

> **People were sitting quietly.** *Some were reading newspapers, some were lost in thought, and some were resting, their eyes closed. It was apparently a calm, peaceful scene. Then suddenly a man and his children entered the subway. The children were so loud and rambunctious that the whole climate changed instantly. People in the subway were distracted and upset.*
>
> *The man sat down next to him and closed his eyes, apparently oblivious to the situation. The children were yelling and throwing things, even grabbing people's newspapers. It was quite disturbing. And yet, while all this was going on, the man sitting next to him did nothing. It was difficult not to feel irritated. Covey could not believe that this man could be so insensitive as to let his children run wild like that and do nothing about it, taking no responsibility as all. It was easy to see that everyone else on the subway felt irritated too. So finally Covey, with what he felt was unusual patience and restraint, turned to him and said, "Sir, your children are really disturbing a lot of people. I wonder if you couldn't control them a little more?"*

(Stop here and lead the class activity described in the margin.)

> *The man lifted his gaze as if to come to a consciousness of the noise for the first time and said softly, "Oh, you're right. I guess I should do something about it. We just came from the hospital where their mother died about an hour ago. I don't know what to think, and I guess they don't know how to handle it either."*
>
> *Covey continues: "Can you imagine what I felt at that moment? ...Suddenly I saw things differently, and because I saw differently, I thought differently, I felt differently, I behaved differently.*

"The greatest mistake is to continue to practice a mistake."
Bobby Bowden

Class Activity
At this point in Covey's experience, stop reading and ask the study group to share some of the feelings and attitudes that they are experiencing about the man and his not doing anything about his children's behavior.

Acknowledge that the information that we have learned so far about this strange event would certainly cause the average person to become irritated and upset with the situation.

You might ask: "Given what he knew and believed to be accurate information as he observed it, was Covey's response to the man a reasonable one?"

After you read the man's answer and Covey's automatic response to the new and enlightening information, ask the study group to respond by expressing their new:

- Thoughts
- Feelings
- Actions they now would choose
- Irritation vanishing
- No longer having to control attitudes and words
- Sympathy and compassion flowing freely because of new insight about the situation as it really is
- The desire to help

My irritation vanished. I didn't have to worry about controlling my attitude or my behavior; my heart was filled with the man's pain. Feelings of sympathy and compassion flowed freely. "Your wife just died? Oh, I'm sorry! Can you tell me about it? What can I do to help? Everything changed in an instant."[7]

As long as we believe incorrectly about God, about relationships, about self-centeredness, about forgiveness, etc., our behavior and our character are being shaped incorrectly. False information does more than lead us to make wrong decisions; it causes us to be the wrong kind of people. So, God's plan is to make us into the right kind of person by changing us from the inside. He knows that what we believe will determine what we *do* and who we *become*.

Our thinking will have to undergo a change as we reflect on the new information we encounter in Scripture. When that happens, we check our current beliefs and leave behind those that we now realize are wrong. Now let's look at some specific areas of character that are difficult to deal with because of a misunderstanding that is often attached to them. In his book *Like A Rock*, Andy Stanley speaks about the lies that we consider to be true. Much of the following discussion is an understanding that comes from his work.[9] We'll see how each lie is corrected by a specific Scripture.

Self-Centeredness

One obstacle that hinders us in building good relationships is **justified self-centeredness**—a selfishness that we feel is entirely reasonable in light of who we are or how we've been treated.[10] The lie that makes this self-centeredness so acceptable is:

> **"If I have a need, then I have the right to satisfy that need."**

A part of the lie is that our needs are more important than the needs of others. Whatever the need is (hunger, rest, favorite TV program), we tend to think that life at home or work revolves around our needs—

not anybody else's. Satan would like for us to continue demanding all this special attention for what we consider to be the right reasons. While we think that our needs should come first, the truth is that there is something more important than meeting our own needs—a right relationship with our Lord and our family. Jesus corrects this self-centered misinformation. He says:

> *"Do nothing from selfishness or empty conceit, but with humility of mind regard one another as more important than ourselves; do not merely look out for your own personal interests, but also for the interests of others."*

> Philippians 2:3-4

While we are all susceptible to this kind of reasoning, if selfishness is a particularly difficult area for you to overcome, it is helpful to write the above verse on a note card and carry it with you in your pocket or purse. Having the truth at hand to counter the lie of self-centeredness is a part of the **training** necessary for character building.

Our training must focus on looking out for others by keeping in mind that people are extremely valuable. Think of them as being <u>more</u> important than we are. Prayer is a part of our training, and by personalizing and praying the words of Philippians 2:3-4, we can gain God's help in firmly establishing this character quality as a part of who we are.

In the block below are the **Basics**. This is important information for **Training Well**. It's just the right amount of information that can be put on a note card to carry with you for memorization. Training is a part of the *JOURNEY*, if you're dedicated.

SELF-CENTEREDNESS

■ *"I have the right to meet my needs."*

■ *"Do nothing from selfishness or empty conceit..."* Philippians 2:3

Note

The **principle** here is that we should correct a specific lie with a specific truth—to correct the lies taught by the world, quote the instruction that comes from our Father in Heaven.

Jesus is our example.

Ask the study group to turn with you to Matthew 4:1-11.

As you read this instructive event together, point out that Jesus responded to Satan's tempting lie with *"It is written...."*

It is Biblical truth that will be our shield against the fiery darts of Satan's lies.

Class Activity

Ask the members to suggest some things that we would do for someone that we were looking out for because we consider them to be very valuable.

Ask them how things went for them today. (And listen while they explain.)

What they suggest will become a training list, which will prepare them for doing well in overcoming selfishness.

Ask them to write this training list in the margin of their workbook.

Class Activity

Ask the study group to think about ways to guard our thoughts. Here are some to start with:

• Select only moral books, movies, conversations, etc. to put into our minds.

• Pray for and forgive others, who have hurt or disappointed us.

Ask them to suggest other ways to control our thought life and write this training list in the margin of their workbooks.

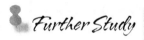

Further Study

Ask the study group to turn to II Corinthians 10:5, where we are told that it is possible to take *"every thought captive to the obedience of Christ."*

Controlling our thoughts is an important part of God's transforming our character by His truth.

Proverbs 23:7 says, *"For as he thinks within himself, so he is."*

Thoughts

We have the idea that our thoughts are completely out of our control. It's like they just come and go from our minds freely, as they wish. The lie is usually stated like this.

> *"I can't help what I think. It 's just there in my mind, and I think about it."*

The truth is that when we are confronted with anger or immoral thoughts, there is something that we can do about it. Through God's grace, we can control what we think about. Our mind does not have to dwell on any immoral or unkind thought that we have. Here is the truth that will counteract the lie about our thoughts.

> *"Set your mind on things above, not on the things that are on earth. For you have died and your life is hidden with Christ in God."*
>
> Colossians 3:2-3

Here is an excellent way to pray at the very beginning of the day. Before you get out of bed in the mornings—before your feet hit the floor and you become concerned with all the thoughts of what you will be facing at work or at home or school—pray for God's help in thinking about the right things. This will protect you from being taken by surprise when temptations confront you. Pray asking:

> *"May the words of my mouth and the meditations of my heart be pleasing in your sight, O LORD, my Rock and my Redeemer."*
>
> Psalm 19:14

THOUGHTS

■ *"I can't help what I think."*

■ *"Set your mind on things above..."*
Colossians 3:2

Honesty

We make use of a lie because we think that it will make us look better by covering up previous bad behavior or pretending to be something that we are not.

"If I change the truth a little bit. I think it will accomplish something for me, now."

The truth is that telling a lie actually opposes the change that God wants to perform in our lives since we've become a believer.

"Do not lie to one another, since you laid aside the old self with its evil practices, and have put on the new self who is being renewed to a true knowledge according to the image of the One who created him..."

Colossians 3:9-10

We are in the process of being "renewed" and that process is hindered when we choose the strategy of telling a lie in order to avoid facing up to consequences or promote our public image.

A good way of <u>training</u> for the character quality of honesty is to practice speaking the truth to everyone.

HONESTY

■ *"Changing the truth a little will help me <u>now</u>."*

■ *"Do not lie to one another..."* Colossians 3:9

Speech

We have been convinced that we have no control over our choice of words when we become angry. The lie about our language goes something like this.

"I just find myself saying all this stuff, and I can't help it."

Ephesians 4:15 tells us to *"Speak the truth in love..."*

Ephesians 4:25 says, *"Therefore, laying aside falsehood, speak truth, each one of you with his neighbor, for we are members of one another."*

Ask the group to list the reference of these verses in the margin of their Bibles beside of Colossians 3:9-10.

If time permits, ask the study group to look up the following references about speaking the truth and list them in the margin of their workbook along with a brief excerpt of what they say.

- Joshua 24:14
- I Samuel 12:24
- II Kings 20:3
- Psalm 51:6
- Proverbs 3:3; 12:17, 19, 22
- Proverbs 23:23
- Ephesians 6:14
- I Timothy 2:7

"Spectacular achievements are always preceded by unspectacular preparation."
Roger Staubach

Don Singleton of Mobile, Alabama said, *"On our first anniversary, after a romantic candlelit dinner, my wife, Elizabeth, emerged from the kitchen with the finishing touch: the top of our wedding cake for dessert. At the first cut, the iced layer 'squeaked' at us. For an entire year, we had saved a round chunk of frosting-covered Styrofoam in our freezer."*[16]

Truth makes a difference, no matter when we find it out.

Note

It has been said that "stuffing our feelings" is unhealthy, and therefore we should express them freely (even anger).

However, we must understand that the opposite of "stuffing" (repressing) our feelings is <u>acknowledging</u> them, not expressing them as many believe.

We *should* acknowledge our feelings and express them to *God.* He wants to hear what is bothering His children. We can express all the hurt and anger to Him and then ask for grace and wisdom to express to our spouse and children only those things that will be edifying (build up).

But God would not have given this command if we were unable to accomplish what He said. Our tongue does not control us.

"Let no unwholesome word proceed from your mouth, but only such a word as is good for edification according to the need of the moment, so that it will give grace to those who hear."

Ephesians 4:29

Our obligation in any relationship is to edify (build up) one another. Abusive language destroys the self-image of those we abuse. It creates hurt and resentment. When we are willing to acknowledge that someone we love has been hurt by demeaning words, and it is our fault; when we see how hurtful our words are, and we are saddened by it, then we will have a new motivation to practice building up the ones we love by the words we speak.

"Death and life are in the power of the tongue..."

Proverbs 18:21

SPEECH

■ *"I can't help what I say."*

■ *"Let no unwholesome word proceed from your mouth..."* Philippians 2:3

Anger

Our abusive or overpowering language is the product of uncontrolled anger. Explosive behavior is expressed because we have been convinced of this lie:

"They deserve it, because of what they did to me."

Most problems in marriage and parenting have to do with anger. It's an issue of self-centeredness. Our focus is on our own irritation or inconvenience. The truth is that in any conflict or power struggle, we should be:

"...quick to listen, slow to speak and slow to become angry, for man's anger does not bring about the righteous life that God desires."

James 1:19-20

Anger expressed in destructive ways, works against God and His plan for you to live a righteous life. Once this undesirable character quality is eliminated, the peace and fun in relationships is unbelievable. Practice for this characteristic involves self-control over expressing our anger in inappropriate ways.

> **ANGER**
>
> ■ *"They deserve it."*
>
> ■ *"...be quick to listen, slow to speak, slow to anger."* James 1:9

Relationships

Although we doubt that we are able to control our thoughts and our speech, we are strangely confident that the friends that we are around most will not exert any real influence over our character. This confidence that we will not be effected by their influence actually makes us much more vulnerable. With our guard down, we are an easy target. Do you recognize the lie?

"They are not going to influence me. I can handle it."

The truth is that we are always going to our friends for advice. We follow that advice most of the time. The Bible says that is dangerous.

"He who walks with the wise grows wise, but the companion of fools suffers harm."

Proverbs 13:20

(continued on next page)

Pick your companions well. They will hold great sway over your character. Their influence is so powerful because of your desire to be accepted, even if it goes against what God wants to do. It's difficult to practice something that we do not want to do. Here's where we must pray for wisdom and strength to train according to His truth, even if we must give up some friendships that would have later caused us to crash.

> **RELATIONSHIPS**
> - *"They're not going to influence me."*
> - *"...the companion of fools suffers harm."*
> Proverbs 13:20

Forgiveness

A major reason for being unforgiving is that we think the other person deserves our resentment and retaliation. Actually, we want them to suffer right now for what they've done so we can observe it. The lie we believe goes like this:

"They don't deserve my forgiveness."

The truth is that God has given us the ability to forgive and it is our obligation, because He has forgiven us.

> *"Be kind to one another, tenderhearted, forgiving each other, just as God in Christ also has forgiven you."*
>
> Ephesians 4:32

As we recall how wonderful it is to have been forgiven by our Father in Heaven, and that His desire is for us to do the same thing, forgiving becomes much easier. Refreshing our mind with the truth of God's forgiveness is part of the training that will prepare us to forgive others. We forgive because we've been forgiven.

(continued from previous page)

Pride ('haughty eyes') tops the list of the most evil character traits. Here are some other references:

- Psalm 18:27
- Psalm 101:5b
- Proverbs 21:4
- Proverbs 30:11-14

> **FORGIVENESS**
>
> ■ *"They don't deserve my forgiveness."*
>
> ■ *"Be kind...forgiving each other."*
> Ephesians 4:32

Pride

We recognize the importance of other people because people are important to God. However, each of us has the ability to think that others are not quite as important as we are. We think that we are better (educationally, culturally, financially, style, looks, brains, etc.). This is a lie that is hard not to believe:

> *"They're OK, but they don't quite measure up to my standard.*

The truth is, if any one is going to boast about anything, God wants it to be that we understand Him and the kind of character He has.

> *"Let not the wise man boast of his wisdom or the strong man boast of his strength or the rich man boast of his riches, but let him who boasts boast about this: that he understands and knows Me, that I am the LORD, who exercises kindness, justice and righteousness on earth for in these I delight," declares the LORD."*
>
> Jeremiah 29:23-24

It is spiritually healthy to be aware of our being special because we are created in God's image. It is also spiritually healthy to be in touch with the fact that we are susceptible to the influence of our old sin nature. None of us have arrived at the point of being perfect, and yet we all have such awesome potential because Christ lives in us. We can *practice* keeping this in mind.

"You have to be willing to out-condition your opponents."
Bear Bryant

Note

The truth of God's Word frees us. Lies actually hold us back from developing godly character into our lives. There is a description in the New Testament about the future of those who *"suppress the truth."*

This description is found in Romans 1:18-32.

Group Activity

Ask the group if they can identify with the following statements. Are there some elements about these statements that are true in your life?

- *"I have had times in my life when I believed certain things about a person, and I acted in a certain way because of my beliefs. Then I found out that what I had believed wasn't true, and after my belief changed, I acted differently toward them. I felt like such a child. After I apologized, we actually became good friends."*

- *"There was a time I thought always of myself. I was determined to put my needs and wishes first. I always got my way. But I badly hurt those that I loved. I know now that I shouldn't have been so selfish. I feel so empty."*

Or maybe there was a time when you were tempted by someone to prove you were a "real man," so, you chose to do something foolish in order to impress them. And when it was all over and you had "proved yourself," you realized what a totally dumb thing you had done, and you thought, *"Why in the world did I do that?"*

> **PRIDE**
>
> - *"They don't quite measure up to my standard."*
>
> - *"...boast...that he understands and knows Me."* Jeremiah 9:24

Compromise

Because we know that God will forgive us when we confess our sins, we might also think that we can avoid the consequences of a moment of compromise (just for a minute, then we will get right back on the right road). That misunderstanding coupled with the wrong idea that we can gain something through a little detour away from devotion to our Lord, will cause our character development great harm.

> *"Look how __much__ I am going to profit by this insignificant little compromise."*

The truth is that this way of thinking will get you into a real mess that will prove to be more costly than you ever imagined.

> *"When desire has conceived, it gives birth to sin; and when sin is accomplished, it brings forth death. Do not be deceived my beloved brethren."*
>
> James 1:15-16

Practice visualizing what horrible effects will be produced by the choice to compromise our integrity or morality. Someone has said that sin will take you further than you want to go; keep you longer than you want to stay, and cost you more than you want to pay.

> **COMPROMISE**
>
> - *"Look how much I am going to gain."*
>
> - *"...sin...brings forth death."* James 1:16

Materialism

If it is your primary goal to have a great paying job, live in a nice house, drive a new car, and wear the best clothes, then you must understand that you will never be content with what you achieve. There is a lie that will direct your life. It sounds like this:

"I will be content as soon as…"

Such a goal can never be satisfied. We will never have "enough." Only God knows what we can handle when it comes to our material possessions. Here's the prayer to train by:

"…give me neither poverty nor riches, but give me only my daily bread. Otherwise, I may have too much and disown you and say, 'Who is the LORD?' Or I may become poor and steal and so dishonor the name of my God."

Proverbs 30:8-9

Train by asking God to give you exactly what He knows is best for you—what you can handle (no more; no less).

MATERIALISM

■ *"I will be content as soon as…"*

■ *"…give me neither poverty nor riches."*
Proverbs 30:8

Change

You don't think you can change because you believe that it's just part of your genes. You inherited it from your Mother or Dad. They were that way too. You'd state this inaccurate perception like this:

"It's just the way I am."

"You play the way you practice. Practice the right way, and you'll play the right way."

Pop Warner

Illustration (Truth)

A former park ranger at Yellowstone National Park tells the story of a ranger leading a group of hikers to a lookout tower. The ranger was so intent on telling the hikers about the flowers and animals that he considered the messages on his two-way radio distracting, so he switched it off. Nearing the tower, the ranger was met by a nearly breathless lookout, who asked why he hadn't responded to the messages on his radio. A grizzly bear had been seen stalking the group, and the authorities were trying to warn them of the danger.[17]

Any time we tune out the **truth** that God is trying to send us, we put at peril not only ourselves, but also those around us. We should never turn off God's true communication.

Additional Scripture

Hebrews 4:16 says, *"Let us therefore draw near with confidence to the throne of grace, that we may receive mercy and may find grace to help in time of need."*

My inherited character doesn't tell me what to look at or where to go or what to say. I control "me" by the power of God. It's my choice.

"I can do all things through Him who strengthens me."
Philippians 4:13

Ask the group to turn to the following Scriptures and list the reference and a brief statement about each verse in the margin of their workbook.

• Ephesians 3:16

• Colossians 1:11

• II Timothy 4:17

Maybe that's what you've always believed, but the truth is, anybody can change! This Scripture is for all believers.

> **"Do not conform any longer to the pattern of this world, but be transformed by the renewing of your mind."**
>
> Romans 12:2

Your heritage has nothing to do with your ability to change. We now have a new birth. You have the Spirit of God living in you. What is the character flaw that you need to change? Ask our Lord to strengthen you as you choose to train by refusing to do wrong. Expressing badness is the biggest obstacle to expressing goodness.[12] Train by practicing the behavioral change that you want to accomplish.

Every lie that influences our character must be corrected by the truth of Scripture. God's grace enables us to stop being controlled by things that are not true. You've now inherited a new nature.

CHANGE

- ◾ *"It's just the way I am."*

- ◾ *"Do not conform any longer...be transformed."* Romans 12:2

Authority

We become frustrated with rules and laws when they don't seem to make sense or when they get in our way and slow us down or prevent things from going our way. Frustrated people express the lie in this way:

> **"If I don't agree with a rule, then I don't have to keep it."**

Guess where that kind of thinking will take you! Actually, God is the Authority behind the laws and authorities that are over us (unless the law is in contradiction to the Scriptures).

"Let every person be in subjection to the governing authorities. For there is no authority except from God, and those which exist are established by God. Therefore he who resists authority has opposed the ordinance of God; and they who have opposed will receive condemnation upon themselves."

Romans 13:1-2

When Paul wrote these words of Scripture, Nero was the emperor of Rome. Israel was under Roman rule. So, we might be able to complain about the decisions made by the Republicans or Democrats, but, if they do not go against the Bible, God expects us to obey them. It's something that we have to train to do consistently.

AUTHORITY

■ *"I don't have to obey, if I don't agree."*

■ *"...be in subjection to the governing authorities."* Romans 13:1

Other Scripture

Obedience to authority is a requirement for those who are selected as church leaders:

"Remind them to be subject to rulers, to authorities, to be obedient, to be ready for every good deed." Titus 3:1

Also ask the students to turn to the following Scriptures and reference them in the margin of their workbook along with a brief summary of what each verse is saying.

• I Peter 2:13

• John 19:11

• Daniel 2:21; 4:17

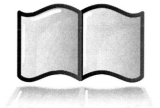

Conclusion

Like a toy wind-up car that tends to curve off to the right or left, we have to be reset for a new start every now and then.[13] We have to depend on truth to let us know when that has to be done, so that our character will end up the way it's suppose to be. We are built with the capability of being spiritually reset.[14]

The world system can be expected to supply us with information that is not true and make it sound so believable. For the rest of our lives here on earth we will be determining the difference between the true and the false.

A lady wrote to the Corpus Christi Caller-Times:

"I was a paid 'screamer' at the first Elvis concert in Dallas... I was working as an usherette for the State Fair Association. All usherettes were called into the office and asked if we would like to earn some extra money. Of course, we all said yes, we

According to Hollywood:

- All grocery shopping bags contain at least one stick of French bread.

- The ventilation system of any building is the perfect hiding place.

- A man will show no pain while taking the most ferocious beating but will wince when a woman tries to clean his wounds.

- Cars that crash will almost always burst into flames.

- It is always possible to park directly outside the building you are visiting.

- Any lock can be picked by a credit card or a paper clip in seconds—unless it's the door to a burning building with a child trapped inside.

- All bombs are fitted with electronic timing devices with large red readouts so you know exactly when they will go off.

- It doesn't matter if you are heavily outnumbered in a fight involving martial arts; your enemies will patiently wait to attack you one by one by dancing around in a threatening manner until you have knocked out their predecessors

These aren't the only ways that movies twist reality. A large part of our beliefs about immorality also are picked up from Hollywood's strategy of making wrong actions seem right.

would. A schedule was set up and we all were paid an extra $10 a night for screaming. Some of us were chosen to faint. The fainters were paid extra.

Elvis appeared before the concert and was introduced to us. We were told to mob him and rip his clothes off. He had a break-away costume designed for the event..."[15]

This all looked real, but it was false (pretend). Once we recognize the truth, then it makes sense to **practice** the fundamentals that will prepare us to **perform** the Christian life with godly character.

CHARACTER PART II

Chapter 5

Train Well and Try Hard

Training Well, as we've just learned, has to do with finding the truth about how life really works, and then practicing what we know for sure to be true. The truth that we encounter in the Bible needs to be clearly understood and deeply established so that it will shape who we truly are. The knowledge of the truth has to be the basis of our practice or else we will never be successful in the process of character building. Darrell Royal, coach of Texas and Mississippi State, said:

"You can't be aggressive and confused at the same time."[1]

We want to have the character to pursue the things that really matter. We don't want to waste time and energy by focusing our effort on something that will not have a lasting impact for God's Kingdom. We don't want to be foolish about choosing the things that we dedicate our life to.

In 1923, a group of the world's most successful financiers gathered in the Edgewater Beach Hotel in Chicago. Even in the fabulous twenties the meeting was an impressive array of wealth and power. Seated at a single table were:

- *the president of the world's largest independent steel company*
- *the president of the largest utility company*
- *the president of the New York Stock Exchange*
- *a member of the cabinet of the President of the United States*
- *the president of the Bank of International Settlements*
- *the man who was known as the biggest trader in Wall Street*
- *the man who headed the world's most powerful monopoly.*

Leader's Prayer

Pray for each member to have <u>great desire</u> to bring honor to Christ through being committed to consistently practicing the attitudes and responses that make him or her successful in building character.

Leader's Plan

Each member of the study group now knows the specific truths that correct the specific lies that usually misdirect our lives.

Now we can encourage everyone to <u>follow through</u> in practicing these important fundamentals.

Parable

The parable, that Jesus told about the rich fool, in Luke 12:16-34, can be applied to these men. Notice especially verses 20-21:

"But God said unto him, 'You fool! This very night your life will be demanded from you. Then who will get what you have prepared for yourself?' This is how it will be with anyone who stores up things for himself but is not rich toward God."

Illustration

We have a responsibility to get a good hold on the truth.

In the 1988 Olympics, the world assumed that the United States would be victorious in the 400-meter relay. They simply were the best.

The gun cracked and they were off and running.

The United States was ahead by 10 meters with no real competition in sight. At the last handoff, the unthinkable happened. They dropped the baton. The thousands in the stands gasped in disbelief.

The United States team— sleek, muscular, and fast as leopards, lost the race.[5]

Truth has been given to us and is intended to be held to firmly and passed on by the influence of our Christian character. We must put the truth of godly character into practice in order to pass it on.

Let's not drop the baton.

Together these men controlled more wealth than the United States Treasury. Their success stories were known to every school boy and girl. They were the models whom other men tried to copy. They were the financial and industrial giants of America.

In 1923 the widely publicized stories of these men were glamorous and exciting. They fired the imagination. They kindled envy. They inspired other men to try to be as they were. But in 1923 their stories were only half-told—the closing chapters were yet to be written.

- *Charles Schwab, president of the steel company, lived the last years of his life on borrowed money and died penniless.*

- *Arthur Cutten, greatest of the wheat speculators, died insolvent (no money to pay debts).*

- *Richard Whitney, president of the New York Stock Exchange, served a term in Sing-Sing penitentiary.*

- *Albert Fall, cabinet member, was pardoned from prison so he could die at home.*

- *Jessie Livermore, the "bear" of Wall Street, committed suicide.*

- *Leon Frazer, president of the Bank of International Settlements, committed suicide.*

- *Ivon Kreuger, head of the world's largest monopoly, committed suicide.[2]*

These men all had money, power, fame, prestige, intelligence, and education, but every one of them lacked the one attribute that gives life real meaning and purpose—dedication to Christ. Their focus was only for this life and themselves. Our focus must be to honor Christ and develop His character, so that others will listen when we tell them the story about our wonderful Savior. Truth enables us to evaluate and discern the difference between the things that are really important in this life and the things that are not.

In Jules Verne's novel, *The Mysterious Island*, he tells the story about five men who escape a Civil War prison camp by hijacking a hot-air balloon.

As they rise into the air, they realize the wind is carrying them over the ocean. Watching their homeland disappear on the horizon, they wonder how much longer the balloon can stay aloft.

As the hours pass and the surface of the ocean draws closer, the men decide they must cast overboard some of the weight, for they had no way to heat the air in the balloon. Shoes, overcoats, and weapons are reluctantly discarded, and the uncomfortable aviators feel their balloon rise, but only temporarily. Soon they find themselves dangerously close to the waves again, so they toss their food. Better to be high and hungry than drown on a full belly.

Unfortunately, this, too, is only a temporary solution, and the craft again threatens to lower the men into the sea. One man has an idea: they can tie the ropes that hold the passenger car and sit on the ropes. Then they can cut away the basket beneath them. As they sever the very thing they had been standing on, it drops into the ocean, and the balloon rises.

Not a minute too soon, they spot land. Eager to stand on solid ground again, the five jump into the water and swim to the island. They live, spared because they were able to discern the difference between what really was needed and what was not. The "necessities" they once thought they couldn't live without were the very weights that almost cost them their lives.[4]

We can no longer carry around the baggage that detracts us from accomplishing our goal of building godly character. The habits and beliefs that are not needed must be thrown overboard. Like the excess weight in the hot-air balloon, living with our old strategies of selfishness, anger, rebellion, etc., can cost us our lives.

In the last chapter, we learned some of the basics to be practiced in the process of building Christian character. Now it's time to put those elements of truth into our performance as we live each day as true friends of our Lord. Our life as a dedicated believer must be focused. We can no longer "just do something" for the sake of activity and adventure. Our goal must become the **performance** of the truth that we have diligently practiced. Just making choices without serious evaluation of our goals will get us in a lot of trouble.

Illustration *(Training has a Purpose)*
Years ago, on "The Merv Griffin Show," the guest was a body builder. During the interview, Merv asked, *"Why do you develop those particular muscles?"*

The body builder simply stepped forward and flexed a series of well-defined muscles from chest to calf. The audience applauded.

"What do you use all those muscles for?" Merv asked. Again, the muscular specimen flexed, and biceps and triceps sprouted to impressive proportions. *"But what do you use those muscles for?"* Merv persisted. The body builder was bewildered. He did not have an answer other than to display his well-developed frame.

Our spiritual exercises— Bible study, prayer, reading Christian books, memorizing, and meditating are all for a purpose. They are meant to strengthen our skill in Christian living, not simply to improve our pose before an admiring audience.[9]

Try Hard & Train Well

Other areas in which the believer is to "make every effort:"

- "To preserve the unity of the Spirit among one another" Ephesians 4:3

- "To gain the approval of God in our understanding of the Scriptures" II Timothy 2:15

- "To enter into the Sabbath rest that the Lord has provided to believers who obey Him" Hebrews 4:11

- "To prepare for His appearing" II Peter 3:14

- "To be certain with respect to His calling" II Peter 1:10

The following story about Larry Walters is true, though you might find it hard to believe. Howard Hendricks tells it this way in his book, *Standing Together:*

> **Larry was a truck driver**, but his lifelong dream was to fly. When he graduated from high school, he joined the Air Force in hopes of becoming a pilot. Unfortunately, poor eyesight disqualified him. So when he finally left the service, he had to satisfy himself with watching others fly the fighter jets that crisscrossed the skies over his backyard. As he sat there in his lawn chair, he dreamed about the magic of flying.

> Then one day, Larry Walters got an idea. He went down to the local army-navy surplus store and bought a tank of helium and forty-five weather balloons. These were not your brightly colored party balloons; these were heavy-duty spheres measuring more than four feet across when fully inflated.

> Back in his yard, Larry used straps to attach the balloons to his lawn chair, the kind you might have in your own backyard. He anchored the chair to the bumper of his jeep and inflated the balloons with helium. Then he packed some sandwiches and drinks and loaded a BB gun, figuring he could pop a few of those balloons when it was time to return to earth.

> His preparations complete, Larry sat in his chair and cut the anchoring cord. His plan was to lazily float back down to the ground, but things didn't quite work out that way.

> When Larry cut the cord, he didn't float lazily up; he shot up as if fired from a cannon! Nor did he go up a couple hundred feet. He climbed and climbed until he finally leveled off at eleven thousand feet! At that height, he could hardly risk deflating any of the balloons, lest he unbalance the load and really experience flying. So he stayed up there, sailing around for fourteen hours, totally at a loss as to how to get down.

Eventually, Larry drifted into the approach corridor for Los Angeles International Airport. A Pan Am pilot radioed the tower about passing a guy in a lawn chair at eleven thousand feet with a gun in his lap. (Now there's a conversation I'd have given anything to have heard!)

The Los Angeles Airport is right on the ocean, and you may know that at nightfall, the winds on the coast begin to change.

So as dusk fell, Larry began drifting out to sea. At that point, the Navy dispatched a helicopter to rescue him, but the rescue team had a hard time getting to him, because the draft from their propeller kept pushing his homemade contraption farther and farther away. Eventually, they were able to hover over him and drop a rescue line with which they gradually hauled him back to earth.

As soon as Larry hit the ground, he was arrested. As he was being led away in handcuffs, a television reporter called out, "Mr. Walters, why'd you do it?" Larry stopped, eyed the man, then replied nonchalantly, "A man can't just sit around."[5]

Now don't get me wrong. I am not saying that "just sitting around" is OK. However, we shouldn't do something stupid in life just to be doing something. We have a purpose for our life, and it would be a terrible loss to allow our years to pass by and never experience doing what God has created us to do. Mike Yaconelli wrote an article in the *Whittenburg Door* years ago that tells about a boy who wanted more than anything else to fight fires.

> **He spent his childhood with this single dream.** *When he was old enough he went to the finest fire fighting school there was. He graduated with honors. One of his professors arranged for him to travel to Europe to study under the finest fire-fighting theorist in the world. He spent two years in Europe and devoted himself to his studies.*
>
> *He finished his studies in Europe and was fully prepared to start fighting fires. He was a bit concerned that other, less trained, fire fighters would endanger him because of the lack of their knowledge of fire fighting. Before he took a job as a fire fighter, he was offered a teaching position to teach others to fight fires.*

Note

The beginning statement of I Peter 1:5, *"For this very reason,"* is a reference to verse 3, which states, *"...His divine power has given us everything we need for life and godliness through our knowledge of Him."* All we need in order to live with godly character has been given to us through the Scriptures, which give us knowledge about God. Now we are to take that knowledge and give all our effort to add character to our saving faith.

So in choosing our character traits, we must look at God's Word for direction. It gives us everything we need.

Other Scriptures speak in terms of an all-out effort being given in order to perform the Christian life well:

• I Corinthians 9:26-27 *"Therefore <u>I do not run</u> as a man running <u>aimlessly</u>; I do not fight like a man beating the air.*
"But <u>I buffet my body</u> and <u>make it my slave</u>, less possibly, after I have preached to others, I myself should be disqualified."

• Philippians 3:14 *"<u>I press on</u> toward the goal to win the prize for which God has called me heavenward in Christ Jesus."*

• Hebrews 6:1 *"Therefore, leaving the elementary teaching about the Christ, let us <u>press on</u> to maturity."*

• Colossians 3:17 *"And whatever you do in word or deed, do all in the name of the Lord Jesus…"*

• I Corinthians 15:58 *"Therefore, my beloved brethren, be steadfast, immovable, always abounding in the work of the Lord…"*

• Deuteronomy 6:5 *"And you shall love the LORD your God with all your heart and with all your soul and with all your might."*

Each of these Scriptures indicates the idea of putting forth great effort in living out our Christian character.

After twenty-five years as he lay on his death bed, he wrote that his passion was always to fight fires. As he looked back at his life, he never had put out a real fire. Never.[7]

Commenting on this same kind of sad ending to a potentially effective life, Winston Churchill said:

"To every man there comes that special moment when he is offered that chance to do a very special thing unique to him. What a tragedy if that moment finds him unprepared."[8]

So, while we are training well, we must perform the second half of the formula for character development by wisely putting into our performance what we have practiced.

Try <u>Hard</u>

Without training according to truth, **Trying Hard** would get us no where. But, since we've been increasing our skill in making the right character qualities a part of our life, we now must *"make every effort"* to bring these qualities into our relationships. Look at II Peter 1:5-7.

> *"<u>For this very reason, make every effort to add to your faith</u> goodness; and to goodness, knowledge; and to knowledge self-control; and to self-control, perseverance; and to perseverance, godliness; and to godliness, brotherly kindness; and to brotherly kindness, love."*

The phrase *"make every effort"* is stated in other translations as *"giving all diligence"* or *"applying all diligence."* All three of these statements make it clear that we are to apply great effort in adding character to our faith. (By the way, you wouldn't tell an unsaved person to do this. Peter is writing to people who are already saved. By *"making every effort,"* we are cooperating with the Holy Spirit, who is at work in our lives.)

We don't passively become mature. Developing the right kind of character requires diligent participation. Someone has said that we don't "luck" our way into spiritual strength.

William Ward wrote *Twelve Guideposts for Living* which emphasize the principle of going beyond what the average believer might do:

"*I will do more than belong . . . . . I will participate.*

I will do more than believe . . . . . I will practice.

I will do more than care . . . . I will help.

I will do more than be fair . . . . . . I will be kind.

I will do more than forgive . . . . . I will forget.

I will do more than dream . . . . . . I will work.

I will do more than teach . . . . . . I will inspire.

I will do more than earn . . . . I will enrich.

I will do more than give . . . . I will serve.

I will do more than live . . . . I will grow.

I will do more than be friendly . . . . I will be a friend.

I will do more than be a citizen . . . . I will be a patriot."[20]

Christian growth will not happen apart from **Trying Hard**, much like a well-trained athlete walks on to the field ready to give it everything he's got, refusing to do anything half-heartedly.

In verse five of chapter one, Peter spreads out seven qualities that we are to get serious about in our daily performance. We'll look at each one separately.

Goodness

"Goodness" ("virtue") refers to "moral excellence." It means to have mastery over our desires. We are to be moral and ethical people.[11] But we are not to have just any average kind of moral character. "Excellence" refers to mastering something. Like a master electrician or a master carpenter are no longer considered to be a journeyman, they have mastered the trade.[12] So, when you place the admonition to "*make every effort*" along side of the character quality of "*moral excellence,*" we see that Peter is talking about something that is far beyond just being average. He is telling us that we are to be a master at living morally. Make it your goal.

"Goodness"

"Goodness" refers to "Moral excellence."[10]

"Don't go to your grave with a life unused."

Bobby Bowden

Memory Verse
II Peter 1:5
(memorize the first 12 words)

(continued on next page)

You will be tempted often to compromise your moral and ethical commitment. Many elements that we encounter each day are designed to entice you to take your God-given desires beyond God-given boundaries.[21]

No one is beyond temptation. Even Jesus was tempted. Talk to the Lord ahead of time as a defense against temptation. Because temptation can happen so quickly, ask for wisdom to avoid being in the wrong places and dwelling on the wrong thoughts.[22]

> *"Do not set foot on the path of the wicked or walk in the way of evil men. Avoid it, do not travel on it; turn from it and go on your way."*
>
> Proverbs 4:14-15

Moral excellence is the first thing that God wants us to add to our faith.

GOODNESS
- *"Moral Excellence"*
- *Becoming masters at living morally*

Knowledge

It is most important for us to understand <u>why</u> we are to do the things we do. Just performing an activity because we have been told to do so is a sure sign of immaturity. If we are maintaining a moral and ethical life because it is included in our set of rules, the ridgedness of such a life will cause our moral stance to degenerate.[13] So, God is telling us to add knowledge to our faith, because it is His plan that we become informed and understand why we are to live morally.[14]

For us to understand why something is the right thing to do, we need to gain specific understanding[15] from God's Word. Our convictions about how to live are rooted in knowledge, so that we can make our decisions based on truth rather than on mere feelings. God's Word is far different from the word of man. The Bible is living and powerful.

It is truth, not opinion. In order to add knowledge to our faith and to have that knowledge working in us to bring about transformation, we must accept the Bible as truth from God Himself.

> *"We also thank God continually because, when you received the Word of God, which you heard from us, <u>you accepted it not as the word of man, but as it actually is, the Word of God</u>, which is at work in you who believe."*
>
> I Thessalonians 2:13

Paul refers to Timothy as one who was *"…constantly nourished up in the words of faith and sound doctrine…"* I Timothy 4:6b

Chuck Swindoll, in his book *Growing Deeper In The Christian Life*, warns that ignorance of God's Word leads us into the prison of superstition, fear, slavery, prejudice and defenselessness.[17] Always find out for yourself. Don't rely on others to do your thinking.

Ravi Zacharias says:

> As we hurry along, scurrying through life, looking for experiences and adventures that will enrich our lives, God is saying to us, 'Here is the treasure. It's right with you, nearer than you ever dreamed.' It's our Bible, and we neglect it at our peril. …What else in your life offers such resources? What else is so valuable?[18]

Would you choose to go to a surgeon, who had decided to stop studying? Neither would I.[18] We must add knowledge to our faith, because God wants us to know <u>why</u> these character qualities are so valuable.

> *"Hold on to instruction, do not let it go; guard it well, for it is your life."*
>
> Proverbs 4:13

Knowledge is the basis for Christian maturity.

(continued from previous page)

Ask the group members to look up the following references in their Bible and record the Scripture reference along with a brief statement from each.

- II Timothy 2:15
- II Timothy 3:16
- John 17:17
- Luke 4:4 (Deut. 8:3)
- Psalm 19:7
- Psalm 119:18

Each person might desire to begin a list of Scripture references on a clear page in the back of their Bible. The list could have a heading such as "Knowledge."

"Don't live on the fading memories of your forefathers. Go out and make your own records, and leave some memories for others to live by."

Dan McGugin

Note

Self-control is also a fruit of the Holy Spirit:

- *"But the fruit of the Spirit is love, joy, peace, patience, kindness, goodness, faithfulness, gentleness and <u>self-control</u>..."* Galatians 5:22-23

Self-control is also a requirement for a church leader:

- *"Now the overseer must be ...self-controlled..."* I Timothy 3:2-7

- *"Since an overseer is entrusted with God's work, he must be...self-controlled..."* Titus 1:7-9

Note

The source of our strength to exercise self-control in saying *"No"* to ungodliness is the **Grace** that God provides when we pray for help during times of testing.

We don't have to:

- let our eyes look at immoral things;

- allow our tongues to say evil, harmful, sarcastic or untrue things;

- let our minds dwell on sin;

(continued on next page)

> **KNOWLEDGE**
>
> ■ *"Specific understanding of God's Word"*
>
> ■ *Understanding why we are to live morally*

Self-Control

Self-control refers to a balanced life of self-discipline, free from harmful extremes.[16] This could include all areas from physical drives to our thought life. There are harmful and sinful behaviors that should be avoided, and exercising wisdom in making those choices is a character quality that offers valuable protection from a shipwrecked life. As in each of the other character qualities, self-control is a choice. This addition to our character goes hand-in-hand with the knowledge of God's Word. At the basis of every lasting conviction is the knowledge of what makes that choice wise and valuable.

But how does self-control fit God's command to be controlled by the Holy Spirit. The Holy Spirit's control is often viewed as outside of us and instead of us. The truth is that the Holy Spirit's control is *through* us by giving us perspective on life through the Word of God.[23] We learn how to respond to life situations through a framework of Biblical truth, producing the fruit of the Holy Spirit. For example:

> ***"Finally, all of you, live in harmony with one another; be sympathetic, love as brothers, be compassionate and humble. Do not repay evil with evil or insult with insult, but with blessing, because to this you were called so that you may inherit a blessing."***

I Peter 3:8-9

Caution! The alternative to self-control is often an attempt to justify our lack of control or complain about our circumstances as a refuge from responsibility.[24] *"Well, if they had treated you the way they treated me, you'd have said the same thing!"* The danger in that kind of rationalization is that it makes us feel justified in not exercising self-control.

God doesn't want to break our will. He wants us to exercise self-control over our will. He wants to instruct our will in wisdom, so we have understanding and therefore *will* to do the right things.[25]

> ## SELF-CONTROL
>
> ■ *"A balanced life of self-discipline"*
>
> ■ *Making wise choices to avoid sinful extremes*

Perseverance

Zane Hodges offers a clear explanation of the urgent need to add this next character quality:

"Clearly the person who cultivates a virtuous life, which is reinforced by knowledge and self-discipline, is well prepared for the worst of times. But in the midst of trial and disappointment he will find his virtue, knowledge and self-discipline all put to the test. Can he maintain his own standards and self-control? What he needs, therefore, is to develop 'perseverance' so that neither Christian character nor conduct is marred or damaged by even the hardest of personal trials."[26]

Have you ever been tempted to quit whenever things get tough? Maybe you've been tempted to quit school or give up on a marriage that is facing difficulties. Or maybe you've been tempted to give up on staying loyal to Christ during times when financial problems seem to never end or your health fails to improve. Those are the training places that God has chosen to build into your life the character of endurance (perseverance). The truth is that perseverance cannot become a part of our character until God has sent us through some hard experiences.[26]

> *"Consider it all joy, my brethren when you encounter various trials, knowing that the testing of your faith produces perseverance."*
>
> James 1:2-3

(continued from previous page)

- use our hands for wrong purposes;

- walk or drive to wrong places.

*"For the **grace** of God that brings salvation has appeared to all men. It teaches us **to say no to ungodliness and worldly passions and to live self-controlled, upright and godly lives in this present age**, while we wait for the blessed hope—the glorious appearing of our great God and Savior, Jesus Christ."* Titus 2:11-13

*"Let us then approach the throne of **grace** with confidence, so that we may receive mercy and find **grace to help us in our time of need**."* Hebrews 4:16

"Don't lose heart when the activity has lost its appeal. Hang on when the fun and excitement fade into discipline and guts." Chuck Swindoll

As we see first hand that God's grace is sufficient and He is faithful to strengthen us and bring us through even the toughest of circumstances, our confidence in God and His plan grows.

Like a seasoned athlete that has played the full sixty minutes and knows what it's like to be exhausted and learns what to expect and how to handle it, we also endure and because of the experience, we have a broader base of understanding. We have more sensitivity to others who are going through the same kind of tough times, and our spirit becomes more teachable and trusting and loyal.

PERSEVERANCE

■ "Faithfulness during the toughest of times"

■ Becoming more reliable and loyal with experience

Godliness

Godliness refers to the great reverence, loyalty and fear of God that should characterize our life.[27] The writer of Hebrews uses the term this way:

"...let us have grace, by which we may serve God acceptably with reverence and <u>godly fear</u>."

Hebrews 12:28

We are to make every effort to possess a deep reverence and awe for God, who loved us and gave Himself for us. This is when Christ becomes Lord of your life.

You want Him to rule over your life. You yield to His rule over your mind, your sexuality, your will. He is invited to rule over your family life and your business and public life. It is the strongest, most loyal commitment to our King that we have ever made. He can now count on us to obey. Commitment to Him characterizes our life. People no longer question what you believe. You set the example, because of your reverence and awe for the only true and living God.

You are no longer ashamed to represent Him and tell His story of redemption to your friends and neighbors. Adding godliness to your faith means that you have committed to a life of honoring your Lord by carrying out the things He has laid out for you in His Word.

As we will soon learn, the last two crowning traits of Christian character are added through an increasing knowledge of our God. This knowledge comes to us as a result of our obedience to His commands. Love for others comes as we love God and serve Him as our Lord. (This is explained under the final character quality, love.)

GODLINESS

■ *"Our loyalty and reverence for God"*

■ *Committing to His rule over our life*

Brotherly Kindness

Brotherly love has to do with how we relate to our brothers and sisters in Christ. There are three verses in I John 3 that tell us how to recognize brotherly love when we see it. The understanding that we have about love comes from Christ Himself. He is our example:

> *"We know love by this, that He laid down His life for us; and we ought to lay down our lives for the brethren."*

> I John 3:16

His love caused Him to take unselfish action in that He *"laid down His life for us."* Brotherly love is a sacrificial kind of love. God's statements of love are supported by actions of love.[29] Statements of love not supported by actions of love is not love at all.[30]

How can we transfer this action to the way we love a fellow believer? Verse 17 makes the application:

Note

The word *"know"* in I John 3:16 refers to definite knowledge that we are taught. We learn by observation, not by experience.

We gain an understanding of what brotherly love really is once we see the kind of love Christ has for us.

I John 4:10,11 puts it like this: *"In this is love, not that we loved God, but that He loved us and sent His Son to be the propitiation for our sins. Beloved, if God so loved us, we also ought to love one another."*

God's love was *"demonstrated."* See Romans 5:8.

Ask everyone in the group to turn to these Scriptures and reference them with I John 3:16.

Note

The word for *"life"* in verse 16 is **psyche**, but in verse 17, John uses another word for life—**bios**, which refers to life in its earthly and material aspects. Therefore, it is translated as *"goods."* The thought in verse 17 is that of sharing with other believers the material things that sustain life. That is a way of *"laying down our lives"* for them. If what might keep me alive is given to a fellow believer who is in need, then I have shown sacrificial love by the actions I have taken. This is the example given to us by our Lord in verse 16.[31]

Note

It is important to be careful in getting our book, chapter and verse reference recorded correctly when listing these Scriptures for future use.

A friend of mine was sending a card of encouragement to his life-long neighborhood friend, who was planning her wedding and was afraid because the whole event was so overwhelming to her.

While my friend signed the card and intended to write the reference I John 4:18, which says, *"There is no fear in love; but perfect love casts out fear,"* by mistake, he wrote the reference John 4:18, which says, *"For you have had five husbands, and the one whom you now have is not your husband…"*

Some mistakes can be devastating!

Scripture

Brotherly love is added to our faith as we are obedient to the truth in God's Word:

"Since you have in obedience to the truth purified your souls for a sincere love of the brethren, fervently love one another from the heart." I Peter 1:22.

"But whoever has the world's goods and sees his brother in need and closes his heart against him, how does the love of God abide in him?"

I John 3:17

Brotherly love involves sharing material things with brothers and sisters who are in need. When someone needs food, clothing, shelter, or medical care, love goes into action. Love is demonstrated by the things we do.

"Little children, let us not love with word or with tongue, but in deed and truth."

I John 3:18

Love is about what we <u>do</u> in these relationships rather that what we <u>say</u>. Anyone can talk a good game. If we "make every effort" to add this character quality to our faith, it will be a consistent, on-going kind of relationship with fellow believers—even to those who disappoint us and are hard to love.

BROTHERLY KINDNESS

- *"Love demonstrated by helping other believers in need"*
- *Following the example of Christ loving us*

Love

This love goes out beyond the circle of our fellow believers; it's a love for the lost. It is the last item on the list of character qualities that are to be added to our faith, so it is the character of a more mature Christian. The fact of love being an aspect of Christian maturity is seen in I John 4:7b.

"…for love is of God; and everyone who loves is born of God and knows God."

Two things can be said of someone who loves: (1) that person is *"born of God and"* (2) he or she also *"knows God."*[32] Notice that being born of God and Knowing God are treated by John as two different things. Knowing God is a task that believers are to be accomplishing.

> **"But grow in grace, and in the <u>knowledge</u> of our Lord and Savior Jesus Christ..."**
>
> II Peter 3:18

Therefore, if a believer does not love, that would indicate that he has not really come to **know** his heavenly Father. The God who saved him **is love**.[33] This is not referring to the saving knowledge of God but rather the experiential (personal) knowledge of God.

Coming to know Jesus is all about Jesus making Himself known to <u>obedient</u> believers. Jesus expressed it just that way:

> **"He who has My commandments and keeps them, he it is who loves Me; and he who loves Me shall be loved by My Father, and I will love him, and will <u>disclose Myself to him</u>."**
>
> John 14:21

Knowledge about God is achieved as we walk a path of obedience. A new believer does not immediately possess the instruction of God's word that he needs. However, when he is taught these commandments and makes them a part of his own character through obedience, it is then that he or she acquires the knowledge of Jesus that He promises.[34]

Love is truly the crowning character trait of Christian maturity. It is added as believers get to know our Savior personally, through obeying His commandments.

> **LOVE**
> - *"Love for the lost"*
> - *Acquiring love by getting to know our Lord*

Note

There is a special sense in which even the Lord's disciples had not known Him.

"<u>If you had known Me</u>, you should have known my Father also: and from now on you know Him and have seen Him."

Philip said to Him, *"Lord, show us the Father, and it is enough for us."*

Jesus said to him, *"Have I been so long with you, and yet you have not <u>come to know Me</u>, Philip?"* John 14:7-9

Philip had already believed in Jesus (John 2:11), but there was knowledge that he did not have, even after being a disciple for three years.

Note

There is a test by which we can see if we have gained any personal knowledge of God:

"Now by this we know that we know Him, if we keep His commandments."

The words *"by this"* are explained by the phrase *"if we keep His commandments."*[35]

"Don't wait to be a great man. Be a great boy."

Shug Jordan

Note

Notice in verse 9 that the believer who lacks these character qualities is:

- *"blind"* (to spiritual truth);

- *"shortsighted"* (about the future return of Christ)— This is a point that Peter stresses: 1:11, 16,19; 3:4-14;

- *"forgetful"* (that he has been cleansed from his sins).

So, we see that a Christian, one who has been "cleansed" from his sins, can be blind, shortsighted, and forgetful regarding spiritual matters, if he refuses to "give all diligence" in adding Christian character to his faith.[39]

Character development is a lot like the process we'd go through in preparation for any skill, whether becoming a concert pianist, a surgeon or an NFL quarterback, the principle is the same. We train by practicing the skills that we will need to use in our performance (in the game, on stage, in the operating room, at home, in school, or on the job).

Results of Character-Building

Any believer who adds character to his or her faith will become an active, fruitful Christian:

> *"For if these things are yours and abound, you will be neither barren nor unfruitful in the knowledge of our Lord Jesus Christ."*

II Peter 1:8

The word **"abound"** means to be "increasing."[37] This is the principle of continuing maturity. We will always need to be growing in our character. The character developing process cannot be a "fad" (a temporary focus on a briefly popular fashion). There should be nothing new that will come along and take its place. Our growth in character cannot even be a "trend." Though a trend is a longer lasting, more sustainable change,[40] we must have something more significant. The character developing process is more dramatic and far-reaching. This transformation, changing us from the inside, should be a life-long process.

"Barren" refers to being "idle, lazy or useless."[38] It has to do with a believer being inactive in his Christian life.

Therefore, through Peter's statement in verse 8, we see that fruitful Christian activity is brought about by ever increasing Christian character. This spiritual growth will not occur automatically. It cannot occur without our **Trying Hard**. Of course our efforts are not all on our own. God supplies the strength through His grace:

> *"And God is able to make all grace abound toward you; that you, always having all sufficiency in all things, may abound to every good work."*

II Corinthians 9:8

Christian character is the oil, which keeps fruitful Christian activity running smoothly. Andy Stanley explains:

The automobile engine is one of the most intricate and elaborate sequences produced by the industrial age. An electromagnet propels a whirling gear into contact with the teeth of the flywheel. The crankshaft propels to 300 rounds per minute. A delicate timing system opens and closes valves. A piston compresses the oxygen and vaporizes fuel trapped in the chamber. The distributor releases a spark at the precise moment of full compression, igniting the fuel like a well-timed lightning strike. The explosion produces enough force to propel a 22-caliber bullet a distance of more than five miles.

Throughout the engine hundreds of form-fitted metal parts begin to grind against one another as the explosions continue.

At 1,200 revolutions per minute, the friction they create causes engine temperature to rise at a rate of seven degrees per second.

The oil pump rushes to bathe the vital components with a fresh supply of oil. It has eleven seconds to lubricate these components.

During these eleven seconds the engine experiences the equivalent of 500 miles worth of wear, as the components assume an abrasive relationship with counterparts.

Without oil, the same parts, which were designed for such precise compatibility, would destroy one another in a matter of minutes. If you don't believe that, just ignore the little amber engine light on your instrument pannel.[41]

The world is like a complex machine made up of millions of people interacting with one another. Christian character is the oil that enables us to be active and fruitful in a world of relationships that inflict wear and tear.

Note

Here are some additional Scripture references, which indicate that God's grace for a believer is referring to strength or enablement to perform ministry or live out the Christian life:

• Romans 12:3; 15:15

• I Corinthians 3:10; 15:10

• II Corinthians 12:9

• Colossians 4:6

• Galatians 3:8

• Ephesians 3:7; 4:7

• II Thessalonians 1:12

• II Timothy 2:1

• Hebrews 4:16

Divide the study group into smaller groups. Assign several Scripture references to each group. Ask each group to look up the Scriptures and report to the class about the purpose for grace as it is stated in each verse.

They might also relate how God's grace has brought them through significant times in their life.

The instructions in the New Testament for dedicated lives are spoken to:

- **Believers**—*"I urge you therefore brethren, by the mercies of God to present your bodies a living and holy sacrifice acceptable to God"* Romans 12:1. This was something these Christian men and women needed to do, otherwise Paul's "urging" them to do so would be unnecessary.

- **Those who had been baptized**—*"And do not go on presenting the members of your body to sin as instruments of unrighteousness; but present yourselves to God as those alive from the dead, and your members as instruments of righteousness to God."* Romans 6:3, 13

- **Those who are indwelt by the Holy Spirit**—*"Or do you not know that your body is the temple of the Holy Spirit who is in you, whom you have from God, and that you are not your own? For you have been bought with a price, therefore glorify God in your body."*

Don't miss the main point: **Saved people are urged to develop Christian character**.

The Main Point

It is all too easy as we read the Bible to miss the <u>main point</u> in the instructions, and therefore not be involved in the process of developing our character through **Training Well** and **Trying Hard**.

Just before Christmas (December 19, 1603), Orville and Wilbur Wright finally succeeded in keeping their airplane aloft for 59 seconds and traveling 852 feet in the air. They rushed a telegram to their sister in Dayton, Ohio. "First sustained flight today 59 seconds. Hope to be home for Christmas." Splashed across the front page of the Dayton newspaper was, "Popular Local Bicycle Merchants To Be Home For Holidays." [36]

The newspaper missed the *main point* of the historic telegram. The main point in developing our character is expressed by Paul when he says:

"Be imitators of me, just as I also am of Christ."

I Corinthians 11:1

So, the main point of our training is to be like Christ in our thinking, speaking, and doing. He wants us to love like He loves, forgive like He forgives, etc.

Timothy (a believer) was encouraged by Paul to pursue the character qualities of:

"righteousness, godliness, faith, love, perseverance, and gentleness."

I Timothy 6:11

Godly character is a requirement for church leaders:

"For the overseer must be above reproach as God's steward, not self-willed, not quick-tempered, not addicted to wine, not pugnacious, not fond of sordid gain, but hospitable, loving what is good, sensible, just, devout, self-controlled."

Titus 1:7-8

It is Christians who are supposed to add these characteristics to our faith, after we are saved. Acquiring all the elements of Christian character in view of our Lord's soon return for us is like preparing for an upcoming trip:

> **There are important things to do** in preparation when we are going away, some happening months in advance. Flights are scheduled; hotels booked; transportation figured out; destination researched. The suitcases must be packed.
>
> Of course, this means catching up on laundry, some new clothes and finding out what the weather is like where we are going. We have to get traveler's checks. Notes are written to the schools. Lists are made with names of people to call "just in case…" The list goes on.
>
> So many arrangements for a small trip. But they are important. When we get there—if all the preparations have been effective—we should be able to enjoy the time away.[3]

We are making arrangements right now to someday take a trip to be with the Lord forever. The uncertain part is that we don't know when the flight leaves. The only luggage we can carry with us is **character**, and the treasure that we have stored up in heaven through obedience to His Word.

> **"For our citizenship is in Heaven, from which also we eagerly wait for a Savior, the Lord Jesus Christ."**
>
> Philippians 3:20

For those who look forward to His appearing, there is a special reward for their life of righteousness:

> **"…the time of my departure has come. I have fought the good fight, I have finished the course, I have kept the faith; in the future there is laid up for me the crown of righteousness, which the Lord, the righteous Judge will award to me on that day; and not only to me, but also to all who have loved His appearing."**
>
> II Timothy 4:6-8

Note

Paul's words in I Cor. 9:24-27 indicate that Godly character is something to strive for, and that there is a prize to be given to all who do.

"Do you not know that those who run in a race all run, but only one receives the prize: Run in such a way that you may win.

"And everyone who competes in the games exercises self-control in all things. They then do it to receive a perishable wreath, but we an imperishable.

"Therefore, I run in such a way, as not without aim; I box in such a way as not beating the air;

"But I buffet my body and make it my slave, lest possibly, after I have preached to others, I myself should be disqualified."

Illustration

"What a person does when he or she is taken off guard is the best evidence for what sort of person they are. If there are rats in the cellar, you are most likely to see them if you go in very suddenly. But the suddenness does not create the rate; it only prevents them from hiding.

"In the same way, the suddenness of the provocation does not make me ill-tempered, it only shows me what an ill-tempered person I am."

—C.S. Lewis

"Transformation"

This refers to a change that is not visible to the physical eye.[4]

Train Well & Try Hard

Someone correctly observed:

• **A good track coach**: *"We can break the record, but this is what it will take…"* Then he gives an awesome workout schedule.

• **A good editor**: *"This work has potential. Here's what we need to cut."* The writer groans as the red ink flows.

• **A good piano instructor**: *"I think you can master this piece for the competition, but to do so, here's our rehearsal schedule."* And the pianist sighs as she sees the hours required.

• **Our truly good God**: *"You can be fruitful, but you'll have to follow My guidelines, if you're going to run with perseverance the race that is set before you."*

(Source Unknown)

There is indeed much for the believer to do. And it will require us to *"make every effort."*

Preparing for that trip to heaven some day requires that we attain to Godly character by being transformed. God's truth, written in the Scriptures, is the instrument that counteracts the lies that we have believed in the past. The truth of Scripture enables ordinary believers to **Train Well** and stop practicing the wrong behavior and strategies that have held us back for so long.

This transformation is something that happens on the inside. And it happens to ordinary Christian men and women, who have become dedicated followers of our Lord Jesus Christ.

Antonio Stradivarius was an Italian violinmaker who lived from 1644-1737. His violins are now the most prized violins ever made because of the rich and resonating sound they produce. The unique sound of a Stradivarius violin cannot be duplicated.

Surprisingly, these precious instruments were not made from treasured pieces of wood. They were carved from discarded lumber. Stradivarius was very poor and could not afford fine materials like his contemporaries. He got most of his wood from the dirty harbors where he lived. He would take those waterlogged pieces of wood to his shop and clean them up. Then from pieces of trashed lumber he would create instruments of rare beauty.

It has since been discovered that while that wood floated in those dirty harbors, microbes went into the wood and ate out the center of those cells. This left just the fibrous infrastructure of the wood that created resonating chambers for the music. From wood that nobody valued, Stradivarius produced violins that everybody wants.[36]

Just as the poor violinmaker transformed trash into treasures, God can and wants to transform every one of us into the treasured image of His Son, Jesus Christ. He can rescue us from the sludge of our sin and transform us into instruments of beauty and grace.[36]

Training Well and Trying Hard involves listening to and obeying the Word of God with earnest dedication.

Robert Kupferschmid, 81, had *no flying experience. In an emergency, however, he learned quickly how to land a plane.*

Kupferschmid and his 52-year-old pilot friend, Wesley Sickle, were flying from Indianapolis to Muncie, Indiana, in June 1998. During the flight, the pilot slumped over the controls. He was dead. The Cessna 172 single-engine plane began to nosedive, and Kupferschmid grabbed the controls. He got on the radio and pleaded for help.

Nearby were two pilots who heard the call. Mount Comfort was the closest airport, and the two pilots gave Kupferschmid a steady stream of instructions, climbing, steering, and the scariest part, landing. The two experienced pilots had Kupferschmid circle the runway three times before the somewhat frantic and totally inexperienced pilot was ready to attempt the landing.

Emergency vehicles were called out for what seemed like an approaching disaster. Witnesses said the plane's nose nudged the center line and bounced a few times before the tail hit the ground. The Cessna ended up in a patch of soggy grass next to the runway. Amazingly, Kupferschmid was not injured.[36]

This pilot listened to and followed those instructions as if his life depended on it, because it did. Imagine what would take place in the lives of believers if we listened to and obeyed the Word of God with the same earnestness.[42]

Maturity

Not, how did he die? But, how did he live?

Not, what did he gain? But, what did he give?

These are the merits to measure the worth of a man as a man, regardless of birth.

Not, what was his station? But, had he a heart?

And how did he play His God-given part?[43]

FRUITFULNESS
IN OUR CHRISTIAN LIFE

Chapter 6

A <u>Successful</u> Christian

Stephen Covey paints an awesome word picture when he asks us to:

In your mind's eye, see yourself going to the funeral of a loved one. Picture yourself driving to the chapel, parking your car, and getting out. As you walk inside the building, you notice the flowers and the soft organ music. You see the faces of friends and family you pass along the way. You feel the shared sorrow of losing and the joy of having known, that radiates from the hearts of the people there.

As you walk down the aisle to the front of the room and look into the casket, you suddenly come face to face with yourself. This is your funeral, three years from today. All these people have come to honor you, to express feelings of love and appreciation for your life.

As you take a seat and wait for the services to begin, you look at the program in your hand. There are to be four speakers. The first is one from your family, immediate or extended—children, brothers, sisters, nephews, nieces, aunts, uncles, cousins, and grandparents who have come from all over the country to attend—one of them will speak.

The second speaker is one of your friends, someone who can give a sense of what you were as a person.

The third speaker is from your work or profession. And the fourth is from your church or some community organization where you've been involved in service.

Leader's Prayer

Pray that as each person considers the parable of the seed and the soils, they will be able to see that not all believers will successfully navigate their way through temptations, worries, riches and pleasures to become mature productive men and women. Only those who, out of a grateful heart, who hold on to God's Word will be successful.

Pray that each member's heart will be neither hard nor shallow nor filled with the pursuit of goals that will blind them to the more important pursuit of Christian character.

Leader's Plan

Allow time for discussion of each written and visual illustration. Plan for time for every one to have opportunity to discuss the scene and interpretation of each of the four kinds of ground (people). Read through the material in this chapter along with any other research well in advance of class time.

The height of your accomplishments will equal the depth of your convictions. *

Ask each member to write down (in the margin of their workbook) their impressions. Ask them to list at least one character trait, achievement or contribution that they desire to be remembered by their:

- Family

- Friends

- Work associates

- Church members

- Neighbors

Give enough time for everyone to list their comments for at least three of the people on the list.

If time permits, ask all volunteers to share some of their choices. Let them know that these choices reflect some of their deep fundamental values.

More Thoughts
(about the end of our life here on earth)

It is also wise to consider what those, who are already in heaven, will say to us (face to face) as we step onto Heaven's shore?

And, most important, what will Jesus, Himself, say about us on that day?

Now, think deeply. What would you like each of these speakers to say about you and your life? What kind of husband, wife, father or mother would you like their words to reflect? What kind of son or daughter or cousin? What kind of friend? What kind of working associate?

*What **character** would you like them to have seen in you? What achievements would you want them to remember? Look carefully at the people around you. What difference would you like to have made in their lives?*[1]

Covey then teaches his famous principle for success: *"Begin everything with the end in mind,"* and advises us to:

> **Begin today with the image** *or picture of the end of your life as your frame of reference by which everything else is examined. Each part of your life—your behavior of each day, each week, each month can be examined in the context of the whole, of what really matters most to you. By keeping that end clearly in mind, you can make certain that whatever you do on any particular day does not violate the criteria you have defined as supremely important, and that each day of your life contributes in a meaningful way to the vision you have of your life as a whole.*[2]

For all of us, who have believed in our Lord Jesus Christ, the criteria that we define as supremely important is *to become like Him and to carry out His great commission.*

Jesus often told the story which explained why people's life ends in success or failure—what kept some from being saved—what kept others from being successful—and what caused others to experience great fruitfulness in their life.

While Jesus was going from one city and village to another healing their sicknesses and diseased and proclaiming the good news about the kingdom of God, great multitudes from these towns were traveling to hear Him. It was to this huge audience along with the twelve disciples and other faithful friends that He taught a parable that had to do *with one's life ending in success or failure.* What He described was a lot like a modern farm setting, with which we are familiar today.

"'The farmer went out to sow his seed; and as he sowed, some fell beside the road; and it was trampled under foot, and the birds of the air ate it up. And other seed fell on rocky soil, and as soon as it grew up, it withered away, because it had no moisture. And other seed fell among the thorns; and the thorns grew up with it, and choked it out. And other seed fell into the good soil, and grew up, and produced a crop a hundred times as great.' As He said these things, He would call out, 'He who has ears to hear, let him hear.' And His disciples began questioning Him as to what this parable might be."

Luke 8:5-9 NASV

Another Parable

Jesus taught another parable that would be good to review as you consider making life choices "with the end in mind."

After your initial discussion of Covey's illustration and what that means to each person in your group, have the members turn to Luke 12:13-34 and read this Scripture about setting our priorities.

Leave time for questions and comments about the kind of goals that we should set for our future.

So, Jesus began to explain the meaning of this story to His disciples:

"Now the parable is this: the seed is the word of God. And those beside the road are those who have heard; then the devil comes and takes away the word from their heart, so that they may not believe and be saved. And those on the rocky soil are those who, when they have received the word

Note

Jesus told this parable on other occasions:

• In Matthew 13:1-23 and Mark 4:1-20 as He sat in a boat at the Sea of Galilee

"Listen to counsel and receive instruction, that you may be wise in your latter days."

Proverbs 19:20 KJV

The Main Point

The issue of the parable of the sower and the soils is the **fruitfulness of believers**.

"One of my goals in life is to wind up with eight men who are willing to carry one of my handles."

Jay Kesler
Being Holy, Being Human

with joy; and these have no firm root; they believe for a while, and in time of testing they fall away. And the seed, which fell among the thorns, these are the ones, who have heard, and as they go on their way they are choked with worries and riches and pleasures of this life, and bring no fruit to maturity. And the seed in the good soil, these are the ones who have heard the word in an honest and good heart and hold it fast, and bear fruit with perseverance."

Luke 8:11-15 NIV

The outcome of our life—whether we were successful or not—depends upon our character. It was the character of the ground that Jesus told about that determined the fruitfulness of the seed that fell there.

The Main Point

To find out what our Lord Jesus is actually saying to us through the words that He has chosen is our primary concern in studying the Bible. If for some reason we miss that message, then we have made a grievous error.

The main point of this parable is that Jesus is teaching the multitudes and the disciples that **He wants everyone who believes in Him to be successful, productive, fruitful disciples. And fruitfulness depends upon the character of each believer in whom God's word is sowed.**

The soil is the character of each individual. Through **Training Well** and **Trying Hard**, the soil in which our lives are growing can be cultivated, weeded, watered and fertilized. Training well involves learning the truth of the Bible by reading, studying and meditating. Trying hard involves obedience to God, obtaining help through prayer, worship with other believers, and reaching out to the unsaved with the good news of the gospel.

The main issue of the parable is whether or not believers are faithful in fruit bearing.

Each different kind of soil represents a person whose character can be observed by his response to God's Word. Let's look at each soil separately to determine how successful they were during their lifetime and *what could be said of them on the day of their funeral.*

SOIL #1—The Roadside

The Scene:

"The farmer went out to sow his seed; and as he sowed, some fell beside the road, and it was trampled under foot, and the birds of the air ate it up."

Luke 8:5 NIV

This is the only soil in which the grain did not germinate and bring forth life. Here the seed did not lodge in the soil; rather it was taken away by the birds. None of it remained to produce a living plant.

The Interpretation:

"Now the parable is this: the seed is the <u>Word of God</u>."

Luke 8:11 NASV

The Word of God has the power to produce life. How many times have we heard through the Gideons (organization) how a Bible placed in a hotel room or a prison was the instrument that brought salvation to someone who was in despair about life.

Paul stated in Romans 10:17:

"...faith comes from hearing the message, and the message is heard through the <u>Word of Christ</u>."

Peter taught those believers, who had been scattered into other countries and cities that:

"...you have been born again not of <u>seed</u> which is perishable but imperishable, that is, through the living and abiding <u>Word of God</u>."

I Peter 1:23 NASV

May I take a moment or two right now to explain something about the power of God's Word. Our solar system has a diameter of 700 light minutes, or eight billion miles. The galaxy, which contains our solar system, has a diameter of 100,000 light years (not minutes). Yet our

Note

It is the **Word of God** that produces life. Here are some verses that show that it is through believing the message about Christ that a person is saved:

- *"And he (Cornelius) showed us how he had seen an angel in his house, which stood and said unto him, Send men to Joppa, and call for Simon, whose surname is Peter; who shall tell you* **words** *whereby you and all your house shall be saved."* Acts 11:13-14

Ask those in your study group to turn in their Bibles to Acts 10:34 and read from 10:34 through 11:1, underlining each time "**word**" is used. John, the apostle recorded in chapter 4:39, 41 of his gospel the fact that:

- *"...from that city many of the Samaritans believed in Him because of the word of the woman who testified, 'He told me all the things that I have done.' ...And many more believed because of His* **Word**.*"*

James wrote in chapter 1 verse 18:

- *"He brought us forth by the* **Word** *of truth, so that we might be, as it were, the first fruits among His creatures."*

Note

In Matthew 13:14, Jesus says that this inability to hear and understand is a fulfillment of the prophesy in Isaiah (6:9).

A description of the people whose hearts were hardened is given in Isaiah 1:1-6 and 5:13-23. They were people who rejected the Word of God.

It would be helpful to reference these verses in the margin of your Bible beside of Matthew 13:1.

galaxy, the Milky Way, is but one of over 10 billion galaxies in the universe.[3] The God in whom we trust is the One who created all this with His **Word**.

> *"By the <u>Word of the LORD</u> were the heavens made; and all the host of them by the breath of His mouth—for He spoke and it was done; He commanded and it stood fast."*
>
> Psalm 33:6,9 NASV

His Word has the power to impart life. That Word is the key part of the parable, which Jesus interpreted to His disciples. His explanation continues:

> *"And those beside the road are those who have heard; then the devil comes and takes away the Word from their heart, so that they may not <u>believe and be saved</u>."*

The *"road"* represents the kind of heart which is a thoroughfare of worldly opinions where the Word of God was *"trampled on"* by a person's own doubts about God's existence or doubts about the promise of eternal life by faith being too easy or too good to be true. In such a heart, the truth could be crushed and taken away by the smooth deception of atheistic professors, who speak with an appearance of intellectual superiority.[4] The Word was taken away, so **salvation did not occur**.

Of the four kinds of ground described by our Lord, this is the only one from which the Word of God was taken away. The birds never touched the seed that fell on the other kinds of ground.

While Satan had *"immediately"* (Mark 4:15) taken away the Word which fell in the road, his act was not against innocent victims. Those represented by the hard roadside are described by Jesus in the same context (Matthew 13:15) as **obstinate people**.

> *"For the heart of these people has become dull, and with their ears they scarcely hear, and <u>they have closed their eyes</u> lest they should see with their eyes, and hear with their ears, and under-*

stand with their heart and return and I should heal them."

So, this ground represents people who have shut their own eyes and ears and hardened their own hearts against God's Word.

In His explanation, Jesus stated that the Devil took away the Word "so that they may not believe and be saved." This agrees perfectly with His statement in John 6:47:

"I tell you the truth, he who believes has eternal life."

Since the Word was taken away before they believed, we know that those represented by the roadside were not saved. The day of their funeral will be a time of sorrow, regardless of the good things they might have done.

SOIL #2—Rocky Soil

The Scene:

"And other seed fell on rocky soil, and as soon as it sprang up, it withered away because it had no moisture."

Luke 8:6

On some farms there are outcroppings of rock that extends out above the surface of the ground. Other farm land might have areas of shallow soil where a slab or sheet of rock is just a few inches below the surface. Either situation would not be sufficient for supplying water for a strong root system, so, the plant would only wither away, therefore it could not produce a crop.

The Interpretation:

"And those on the rocky soil are those who, when they hear, receive the Word with joy; and these have no firm root; <u>they believe</u> for a while and in time of temptation fall away."

Luke 8:13

Other Scripture

Other verses which state that salvation is by faith (believing):

- "<u>Believe</u> on the Lord Jesus Christ, and you shall be saved..." Acts 16:31

- "He who <u>believes</u> in Him is not judged; he who does not <u>believe</u> is judged already, because he has not <u>believed</u> in the name of the only begotten Son of God" John 3:18

- "...for a pattern to them which should hereafter <u>believe</u> on Him to life everlasting" I Timothy 1:16

Note

The term *"joy"* is never used in the New Testament to describe a superficial and insincere excitement.[5] Here are several ways Luke uses this word:

- The joy of Christians because their names are written in Heaven— Luke 10:20

- The joy our Heavenly Father feels when He finds one of His lost sheep— Luke 15:4-7

- The joy of the disciples after Jesus blessed them, just before the ascension—Luke 24:50-53

Additional Scriptures

Other occasions when the phrase *"received the Word"* is used to describe the salvation experience: Acts 2:41; 8:14; 11:1.

Life Exists!

Evidence of Maturity

There are several key observations which Jesus makes about people who are in the rocky soil category. He sees it as important to let us know from the start that these people *"received the Word."* This is a phrase that Jesus knew would be used by the writers of the New Testament to refer to saving faith. Here's how Luke describes the way the people of Berea responded to God's Word.

> **"Now these were more noble-minded than those in Thessalonica, for they <u>received the Word</u> with great eagerness, examining the Scriptures daily, to see whether these things were so. Many of them therefore believed, along with a number of prominent Greek women and men."**
>
> Acts 17:11-12

Jesus adds support to the meaning of *"receiving the Word"* when He states that those represented by the stony ground *"believed for a while."* In verse 12 He had explained that if that group had *"believed"* then they would have been *"saved."* There is no other reasonable conclusion than that the rocky soil people did experience **saving faith**. The phrase *"for a while"* is explained very well by Robert Wilkin as he tells about a present day event that we can relate to:

> **Linda was driving down the freeway** with her radio tuned to a Christian station. She heard the gospel clearly proclaimed and joyfully received the message, believing in Christ for eternal life. Tragically, one minute later, a drunk driver crossed the median and hit her. She died instantly.

He then explains that most would agree that Linda went to Heaven, since she had believed in Christ. Eternal life is granted to a person *at the very moment of faith.* It isn't bestowed after you have believed for a certain length of time. When you place your faith in Christ for eternal life, you are born again right then.

> What if instead of dying in that car accident, Linda had been badly hurt and subsequently became very depressed? Eventually, she even began to doubt that Christianity was true. How could it be true, when God had let this happen to her: If she had

died in this state of unbelief and bitterness, where would she go—to Heaven or Hell?[6]

The truth is that there is no minimum time requirement for believing the gospel. The Greek verb for "believe" is stated in a tense that refers to a *one-time-act*. Believing in Jesus Christ is an event, not a process. Linda or any other person who believes in Christ would go to Heaven at any time after the event of their faith in Christ. So, when Jesus says that they *"believed,"* the conclusion must be that this group was saved.

This understanding is confirmed when Jesus explains in setting the scene in verse 6 that this seed *"sprang up."*

> **"And other seed fell on rocky soil, and as soon as it <u>sprang up</u>, it withered away because it had no moisture."**

Luke 8:6

Only a seed that has germinated and has *life* can *"spring up."* The presence of *life* is shown by the growth that took place.

Jesus is warning believers that it is possible for a Christian to add nothing to their faith and therefore not grow to maturity. The stony ground kind of people become discouraged when hardship comes their way. Rather than seeing the testing as a time to become stronger and wiser and develop perseverance, they become bitter because they have not studied the Scriptures to understand that this is God's plan to bring us to maturity. They are weak because they did not have the nourishment that comes through the insight they would gain from corporate worship, fellowship, and Bible study.

One who does not become mature does not become fruitful. This person would also have some sad commentary on the day of his funeral when family and friends gathered at the Chapel in memory of him and his contributions, character, and achievements.

Here on the rocky soil the *"temptations"* (testing) of life have caused the new believer to *"fall away"* <u>from progressing to maturity and bearing fruit</u>. They were *saved* but never became a faithful follower.

There is a third kind of soil where the warning comes regarding the potential of failure for a different reason. Again it is the issue of discipleship and fruit bearing that Jesus is stressing.

Note

John the Baptist was a believer in Jesus Christ, however when he was placed in prison, he (of all men) also began to doubt and sent some of his disciples to Jesus to ask: *"Are You the Expected One, or are we to look for another?"* Luke 7:19

Even the greatest of believers can have doubts, but our doubts are answered by the Words of Jesus.

Note

In II Peter 1:10, Peter warned believers that, *"...as long as you practice these things (the character traits listed in chapter one verses 5-7) you will never stumble."*

Later at the end of his epistle, Peter stated, *"...be on your guard, lest being carried away by the error of unprincipled men, you fall from your own steadfastness."* II Peter 3:17

Keep in mind that these warnings are given to Christians, because it **is** possible for a believer to be unfruitful and consequently fail to live a life that glorifies God.

SOIL #3—Rocky Ground

The Scene:

"And other seed fell among the thorns; and the thorns sprang up with it, and choked it out."

Luke 8:7

The memory of my high school years, when I went hunting on my Uncle's farm, is filled with experiences of going through briar patches in and along the borders of some of his large grain fields and pastures. Many farmers can relate to the extra expense and work it takes to minimize the destruction that thorns and weeds can cause to their crops. They are wiry things that just over power other plants and take their strength away. This is the third scene that Jesus is describing to the multitudes who have gathered to hear His words.

The Interpretation:

"And the seed which fell among the thorns, these are the ones who have heard, and as they go on their way they are choked with worries and riches and pleasures of this life, and bring no fruit to maturity."

Luke 8:14

Well, the seed that fell among the thorns did *"spring up,"* but it was in a bad neighborhood. This seed had not withered away, like the ones that fell on the rocky soil. These lasted longer and were a little more healthy, but their growth was stunted. The thorns took most of the strength away from these stalks of grain.

Jesus gets more specific here as He identifies the thorns as *"worries, riches and pleasures of this life."* The lives of these people are so crowded with other things that there is no room left for God's Word to really have an impact on them. God's plans had not been honored and given a place of preference. His discipleship program cannot be placed *"with"* our other concerns.

This group of folks produced fruit to a certain state, but they *"bring no fruit to maturity,"* because other things that they desired more took over, and used up their time and energy. On the day of their funeral, you could say many exciting things that they had accomplished and that they were very successful in the eyes of the world, but there would be no precious memories about the influence that God's Word had in their life.

SOIL #4—Good Ground

The Scene:

"And other seed fell into the good ground, and grew up, and produced a crop a hundred times as great."

Luke 8:8

The character of the people represented by *"good ground"* was far different from the others that Jesus had described. This ground was well prepared and very receptive to the same seed that others had rejected, ignored and undervalued. The crop was therefore amazingly fruitful.

The Interpretation:

"And the seed in the good soil, these are the ones who have heard the Word in an honest and good heart, and hold it fast, and bear fruit with perseverance."

Luke 8:15

The thing that made this group so different was the grateful attitude of their hearts. While the believers that Jesus previously described still had hearts that were hard, shallow, and crowded, the group He is now describing considered God's Word to be very valuable, therefore they chose to *"hold it fast."* It was this choice that brought about transformation in their character and fruitfulness in their lives.

Instead of falling away in times of testing, or getting caught up in the busy-ness of life this group was characterized by *"perseverance."*

Because they valued truth rather than buying into the lies that hold us back from developing character, the *"good ground"* people were able to **Train Well**. And because they practiced the truth that they believed to be supremely important, they could make every effort in **Trying Hard** and therefore *"produce a crop a hundred times as great."*

Note

Their choice to *"hold it fast"* was the clear indication that these people had become **disciples** of our Lord:

- *"Even as He spoke, many put their faith in Him. To the Jews who had believed Him, Jesus said, 'If you hold to My teaching, you are really My disciples. Then you will know the truth, and the truth will set you free.'"* John 8:30-31

Remember in chapter 5 we learned that the truth of God's Word can set us free from the lies that always held us back from growing in godly character? Well, this group of people represented by the *"good ground"* **Trained Well** by allowing the truth of God's Word to direct their thinking, choices and actions.

Fruit is Evidence of Maturity

Note

Partial dedication is like:

- a fireman, who responds to a three alarm fire by saying, "It'll probably burn itself out soon enough,"

- or a policeman who, upon arriving at the scene of a robbery, merely shakes his head and says, "Boys will be boys."

- or a doctor, who upon discovering you have a tumor buried deep in your body, responds, "Take two aspirin and you'll be just fine."[7]

On the day of their funeral their family and friends will remember their love of God and His Word and how their lives exhibited the godly character that influenced the whole family beyond imagination. Their fellow-workers will offer testimony to the fact that they walked the same as they talked. Church members will describe them as leaders worth following. Thousands someday will express gratitude to these faithful disciples because they first heard the good news about eternal life from them.

To have a successful life of fruitfulness is possible for every believer, because God:

> **"...has granted to us everything pertaining to life and godliness, through the true knowledge of Him who called us to glory and virtue."**
>
> II Peter 1:3

It's equipment that all believers are given for the *JOURNEY*.

Fruitfulness comes to the believer who perseveres in a life of godly character. Persevering is like "abiding," which we talked about in chapter 2. Both have to do with being an obedient disciple, making the decision to become fully dedicated to Christ.

Ivan the Great sent his counselors and advisers to search the capitols of Europe to find an appropriate wife for the great tsar. And find her, they did. They reported to Ivan of the beautiful dark eyed daughter of the King of Greece. She was young, brilliant, and charming. He agreed to marry her sight unseen.

The King of Greece was delighted. It would align Greece in a favorable way with the emerging giant of the north. But there had to be one condition, "He cannot marry my daughter unless he becomes a member of the Greek Orthodox Church." Ivan's response, "I will do it!"

So, a priest was dispatched to Moscow to instruct Ivan in Orthodox doctrine. Ivan was a quick student and learned the catechism in record time. Arrangements were concluded, and he made his way to Athens accompanied by 500 troops, which formed his personal palace guard.

He was to be baptized into the Orthodox church by immersion, as was the custom of the Eastern Church. His soldiers, ever loyal, asked to be baptized also. The Patriarch of the Church assigned 500 priests to give the soldiers a one-on-one catechism crash course. The soldiers, all 500 of them, were to be immersed in one mass baptism. Crowds gathered from all over Greece.

Can you imagine what a scene that must have been, 500 priests and 500 soldiers, a thousand people, walking into the blue Mediterranean? The priests were dressed in black robes and tall black hats, the official dress of the Orthodox Church. The soldiers wore their battle uniforms with all their regalia and their weapons of battle.

Suddenly, there was a problem. The Church prohibited professional soldiers from being members; they would have to give up

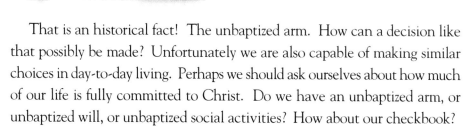

their commitment to bloodshed. They could not be killers and church members too.

After a hasty round of diplomacy, the problem was solved quite simply. As the words were spoken and the priests began to baptize them, each soldier reached to his side and withdrew his sword. Lifting it high overhead, every soldier was totally immersed—everything baptized except his fighting arm and sword.[8]

That is an historical fact! The unbaptized arm. How can a decision like that possibly be made? Unfortunately we are also capable of making similar choices in day-to-day living. Perhaps we should ask ourselves about how much of our life is fully committed to Christ. Do we have an unbaptized arm, or unbaptized will, or unbaptized social activities? How about our checkbook?

If we're going to be fruitful, we've got to be a fully committed follower of Jesus Christ our Lord.

"If I do not practice one day, I know it. If I do not practice the next, the orchestra knows it. If I do not practice the third day, the whole world knows it."[9]

Paderewski

"Take hold of instruction; do not let go. Guard her, for she is your life."

Proverbs 4:13

Most everyone born before 1980 can remember the great tragedy of January 28, 1986.

> **The Space Shuttle Challenger exploded** *just after takeoff, killing all seven astronauts. Although everyone knows that the nature of this disaster was caused by one O-ring, the fate of these astronauts has not yet been publicly defined. Exactly what killed these men and women will probably remain a secret, but it is known they did not die instantly.*
>
> *A recording of their last moments confirms they had time to understand the magnitude of what occurred. This audio transcript reveals a great contrast between the two women on board.*
>
> *Judith Resnik was known for her proficiency but not her faith. Her voice can be heard spewing desperate profanities in the final seconds of her life.*
>
> *Christa McAuliffe was the schoolteacher who did not hide her commitment to God. The same recording includes her partial recitation of Psalm 23.*[10]

One woman met death with desperate curses on her lips while the other entered eternity quoting God's Word. One can hardly imagine a more frightening death, yet Christa McAuliffe's greatest legacy is that of showing us that faithfulness in the face of the most frightening moments of life is possible.

All believers have every thing we need for a successful life of fruitfulness. The choice is ours to do something with what Christ has given us to work with. There must be a time in our lives when we make the conscious decision to become obedient fruitful followers of Christ. For every new believer our Lord has planned a very special event by which we are to identify our selves as a follower of Jesus Christ. Let's look at some details of that occasion.

Baptism
The Sacred Act Of Identification

If we plan to be the *"good ground"* kind of believers, our first act of obedience after we become a Christian is to identify ourselves with Christ and His plan for our life of fruitfulness.

Our Lord had chosen the tangible, physical, public act of baptism as the event that uniquely marks us as followers of Jesus Christ. Special public events are not new to us. We value several such occasions very highly. Much of our time and money goes into a select few special events in our life. Among these are our wedding, our graduation from high school and college, our commissioning into the armed forces, etc. These mileposts are well planned because we want them to show forth their importance as hallowed events of our life. We have them well documented in our photo albums, and we often review them with much pleasure as we turn through the pages of memory. They are statements about who we are.

But these important events, hallowed as they are, pale in significance to those sacred acts that are filled with eternal significance because God, Himself has deemed them holy.[11]

There are only two acts like this that have been set apart by God as sacred. These two rites are *instituted* by our Lord in the Gospels, *practiced* by the Apostles in the book of Acts, and *explained* by the epistles in the New Testament.[12]

One of these events is the Lord's Supper (which we discussed in chapter 3). Our Lord Jesus instituted that event on the night He was betrayed (I Corinthians 11:24-25). The second special event was baptism. Right before His ascension, Jesus commanded that we baptize disciples in all nations.

> *"Go therefore and make disciples of all the nations baptizing them in the name of the Father and of the Son and of the Holy Spirit, teaching them to observe all that I commanded you; and lo, I am with you always, even to the end of the age."*
>
> Matthew 28:19-20

Just to know that Jesus Christ, who loved us and gave Himself for us, commanded these two sacred acts is enough to cause me to want to be a part of His special events for my life. Baptism is something that is so awesomely important. Just as faith in Christ for salvation is a one-time-act, we are only baptized one time. It ought to be done right away, otherwise we are not obedient.

So, let's learn more about baptism. The meaning of the word "baptize" is to *dip, immerse, plunge, sink, or drench*.[13] But more importantly, this

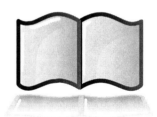

Memory Verse
Matthew 28:19-20

Note

It is safe to say that the Israelites didn't get wet at all when they crossed the Red Sea:

• *"Then Moses stretched out his hand over the sea; and the LORD swept the sea back by a strong east wind all night, and turned the sea into dry land, so the waters were divided. And the sons of Israel went through the midst of the sea on the dry land."* Exodus 14:21-22

sacred act is meant to **identify** us with Christ. It is about identification—that's why it's so sacred.

Arthur Farstad writes about baptism making this identification statement with the following explanation.

> *In I Corinthians 10:2, we read that the children of Israel were "baptized into Moses…in the sea." What does this mean? Were they immersed in the Red Sea? Certainly not. Did it pour on them as they passed through? No. Were they at least sprinkled by the sea? Not even that. By going through the sea on dry land, they were identified with their deliverer, Moses, who, under God, "saved" them from Pharaoh and the armies of Egypt.[14]*

The unbelievable opportunity to be marked out by a public event as followers of Christ is without a doubt the most hallowed of all the special occasions that we cherish so much. I am so glad that I can look back to that special time and place. It was my first step in preparing my heart to be gratefully receptive to His Word.

MAKING DECISIONS

Some Biblical Guidelines

Do you think that God wants us to become consistent in making wise and mature decisions? If we have dedicated our life to accomplish some worthy objective, would God want us to be able to choose the best way to accomplish it? Does God make our decisions for us, or does He desire that we, as His ambassadors, develop skill and knowledge for the decisions that we make in His name?

When our children were small, they required detailed supervision. Deciding things for them and teaching the reason behind our choices was a necessary part of their training. Later on we gave them the responsibility for basic choices that a child of their particular age should be making. As time went by their knowledge and wisdom developed along with added responsibility. We gave our kids more choices, within certain limits. The older they got, the less we told them what to do. We wanted them to practice doing what they would later be expected to do well. Of course consequences were explained and carried out for pre-planned bad choices.

Our children learned the guidelines that we considered valuable. We didn't train our children to ask us what to do every time they were confronted with a choice. That's not the way we wanted them to function as adults. They must learn responsibility and fully understand the meaning of accountability.

They were taught biblical principles and commands and how that was a basis for close friendship with our Creator and Savior.

Discerning between right and wrong, evaluating consequences, honoring parents, and respecting people as being fellow image-

Leader's Prayer

We must pray for wisdom for all those in the study group to see the wisdom of making decisions based on the guidelines given in the Bible. Pray that tradition will not over rule Scripture.

A number of the members of this study group will have had experience in making decisions based on emotions rather than solid facts. So, pray for them to see clearly what our Lord had in mind by requiring us to become good at making mature choices in life.

Leader's Plan

Read through the material for this chapter carefully. Be ready to give examples from your own personal decision making experience (not too many).

Allow time for discussion, and provide a friendly atmosphere and room for other points of view—this is new for a number of those in your study group.

"He who is faithful in a very little thing is faithful also in much; and he who is unrighteous in a very little thing is unrighteous also in much."

Luke 16:10

Note

Choices and conse-
quences are a part of
God's plan for our training
to become mature, adult
Christian men and women:

- "...each one should be
  fully convinced in his
  own mind"

- "...we shall all stand
  before God's judgment
  seat."

- "So then, each of us will
  give an account of
  himself to God."

Romans 14:5,10,12

Note

The Christian life is a
JOURNEY. That's why it is
referred to as a "walk." We
don't get to where we're
going in one giant step.

bearers are only a few of the relational skills that we wanted our children to develop in order to become mature adults.

Of course, the day came when each of them faced choices that would shape their whole life; who to date, what college or university to attend, what career to pursue, who to chose for a marriage partner. The joy is in the freedom to make these choices. We prayed for them and offered advice, when they asked. We assured them that God would honor any decision they made within His moral boundaries.

We would have never been comfortable with this season of their life, had they not had all the previous years to practice for it.

We enjoyed seeing each one of our children make their own decisions. We are still very much involved in their lives, but we no longer tell them what to do.

These years are special because we have confidence in their maturity and dedication to godly principles. Our heavenly Father is also training His children to make good decisions. Of course that involves a great deal of practice. Decision making is our responsibility. Gaining wisdom and understanding is a part of the process, so let's find out how people in the Bible made decisions.

Two Guidelines For Making Choices
1—Honor our heavenly Father

The sure and solid foundation for making decisions is the principle stated by God Himself. Jesus stated this purpose behind the choices He makes:

> "...the Father has not left Me alone; for I do always those things that please Him."

John 2:29

He also advised you and me to embrace the same mindset in our own decisions.

> "Seek first the Kingdom of God and His righteousness, and all these things shall be added unto you."

Matthew 6:33

It is safe to say that, if we learned to think like our Lord Jesus Christ and place this priority into our decision making formula, we'd be making some wise choices. It is certain that we are not to leave God out of our reasoning process. Paul gave this advice to the believers at Ephesus.

"This I say therefore, and affirm together with the Lord, that you walk no longer just as the Gentiles also walk, in the futility of their mind, being darkened in their understanding, excluded from the life of God, because of the ignorance that is in them, because of the hardness of their heart."

Ephesians 4:17-18

2 —Consider The Interests Of Others

We are to make decisions in our daily life with the "same mind that was also in Christ Jesus." Paul explains what exactly this "mind" (attitude) is as he writes to the Philippians.

"Do nothing from selfishness or empty conceit, but with humility of mind let each of you regard one another as more important than himself; do not merely look out for your own personal interests, but also for the interests of others."

Philippians 2:3-4

So, there is our second reason. An astounding principle of decision making is to have the same attitude of humbly looking out for others as well as ourselves.

Let both principles stand like two giant mountain peaks as we seek to determine our direction in life.

1. Always do those things that honor (please) our heavenly Father.

2. Have the same attitude as Jesus Christ, who humbly *considered the interest of others.*

In May of 1996, one of the greatest tragedies in mountain climbing history took place upon the slopes of Mount Everest.

Note

Paul states clearly the reason behind his choice to be a servant of Christ:

• *"Am I now trying to win the approval of men, or of God? Or am I trying to please men? If I were still trying to please men, I would not be a servant of Christ."* Galatians 1:10

Illustration

It was a 99-degree September day in San Antonio, when a 10-month-old baby girl was accidentally locked inside a parked car by her aunt. Frantically the mother and aunt ran around the auto in near hysteria, while a neighbor attempted to unlock the car with a clothes hanger. Soon the infant was turning purple and had foam on her mouth.

It had become a life-or–death situation when Fred Arriolal, a wrecker driver, arrived on the scene. He grabbed a hammer and smashed the back window of the car to set her free. Was he heralded a hero?

"The lady was mad at me because I broke the window," Arriola reported. "I just thought, 'What's more important—the baby or the window?'"

Most questions of priority are not between something important and something trivial; rather they are between the important and the most important.[34]

Note

If the governing authorities establish laws, which demand that we dishonor our Lord or live in a manner, which is in violation of His Word, then we must honor God over and above those laws.

But Peter and the apostles answered and said, "We must obey God rather than men." Acts 5:29

In a quest to stand upon the 29,028 foot summit, twelve climbers lost their lives. Jon Krakauer was a part of this expedition and has written of the experience in his best-selling book, Into Thin Air. Krakauer describes how the imperiled group came to this dreadful fate.

On their final ascent to the top, several climbers violated clear instructions to not be on the summit after 2:00 PM. This delay caused the entire group to remain in a dangerous sector of the mountain for too long. A murderous storm blew in on the climbers and they found themselves in a fight for their lives. The full-blown blizzard sent the wind-chill factor plummeting 100 degrees below zero. They were enveloped in darkness and blowing snow. Visibility dropped to less than 20 feet. Their oxygen was depleted and the batteries on their lights were fading. For two hours they simply staggered blindly through the snow hoping to stumble upon the camp.

Hypothermia and exhaustion were taking a terrible toll, and their floundering steps nearly took them over the precipice of a 7000-foot cliff. Nothing but chaos could describe their search for safety. While the fierce wind continued to create a ground-blizzard, the sky above began to clear. Though twelve climbers had lost their lives, several others looked up, and saw the silhouettes of Everest and Lhotse. From that brief glimpse of these reference points, they were able to determine the route back to camp, safety, and survival.[31]

When the landscape around us is swirling, and the winds of confusion are howling, we can always look to the two reference points of (1) Honoring God and (2) Humbly considering the interest of others for dependable guidance in making decisions. They will lead us to safety and survival.

Of course, all decisions need to follow clearly stated principles and commands in Scripture that are written for the purpose of guiding us in making decisions. For example, our response to the laws of government is spelled out in Romans. So if you have wondered what decision to make about stopping at a stop sign or returning your books to the library on time, read this.

"Let every person be in subjection to the governing authorities. For there is no authority except from God, and those which exist are established by God. Therefore he who resists authority has opposed the ordinances of God; and they who have opposed will receive condemnation upon themselves."

Romans 13:1-2

"Artful Eddie," slickest of the slick lawyers and crony of Al Capone, lived on the wrong side of the law for many years. He would fix dog races by having someone feed all the dogs except one, and then bet on that dog that was not too full to run well. Eddie made the decision to cooperate with the governing authorities and appear as a witness in the trial against Al Capone.

In return for testifying against the mob, the Chicago police agreed to give protection to Eddie's son, Butch and to grant him an appointment to Annapolis, when he graduated from school. The authorities kept their word, and after graduating from Annapolis, Butch was commissioned as a World War II Navy pilot. He was assigned to the carrier Lexington. On February 20th, 1942, when the ship came under attack from nine Japanese planes, with only one fighter plane available for defense, Eddie's son shot down five Japanese planes in five minutes, saving the lives of hundreds of crewmen. The other four planes managed to escape. This event was recognized by the President as the most heroic act of air to air combat in the history of our country, and Butch O'Hare was given the Congressional Medal of Honor. He was later killed in action.[32]

Now when people say the name O'Hare in Chicago—they don't think of gangsters but aviation heroism, because Eddie O'Hare did what was right according to the governing authorities, and that was honoring to God, who established them.

There are numerous statements of Scripture that are solid guidelines for decision making in areas of morality. Here's a good one:

Note

Ask the group members to turn with you to I Thessalonians 5:12-22.

Ask the group to list the specific instructions given in each verse. These can be listed in the margin of their workbook.

• Appreciate church leaders—5:12

• Live in peace with one another—5:13

• Warn the unruly; comfort the fearful; help the immature—5:14

• Do not repay evil for evil—5:15

• Rejoice always—5:16

• Pray always—5:17

• Give thanks for everything—5:18

• Do not quench the Spirit—5:19

• Do not despise prophetic gifts—5:20

• Test everything; hold to that which is good—5:21

• Abstain from every form of evil—5:22

Of all the instructions listed, ask the group to count how many are quite clear and easy to understand. Challenge the study group to keep a running list (as they read their Bible each day) of Biblical commands that give specific guidance for making decisions.

Someone might ask:

II Corinthians 5:7 says that we are to *"walk by faith, not by sight."* How does that relate to decision-making?

Answer:

"Walk by faith" means to live our lives by relying on the truth that God has revealed in His Word. This would include what He has revealed about how His apostles made decisions in situations where God had not given a specific command.

Making Decisions

1. Pray (ask God for wisdom)
2. Research
3. Evaluate
4. Decide

"If any of you lacks wisdom, let him ask of God, who gives to all men generously and without reproach, and it will be given to him."

James 1:5

"For this is the will of God, your sanctification; that is, that you abstain from sexual immorality."

I Thessalonians 4:3

In his book, *Decision Making & the Will of God*, Gary Friesen tells how he had studied long and hard, and felt that he had a good grasp of the material, as he entered the class room.

> **The exam was taxing**, but it was a fair test of how much we had learned. I knew I had done well; the only question was whether I would get an "A" or a "B."
>
> I lived with the suspense for a week or so. At last, the graded exams were returned—the moment of truth had arrived. Or had it?
>
> What was the letter in the upper right hand corner? It was a "D"! How could that be?...I had put a "T" or "F" in each answer blank, while the instructions had specifically directed me to spell out "True" or "False." The penalty never did seem completely fair to me, but I did learn a valuable lesson: Before you begin an exam, read all the instructions carefully.[33]

Much of the following discussion about decision making comes from the understanding that I gained through Chuck Smith, a very knowledgeable friend and professor at Grace Theological Seminary and Gary Friesen, the author of *Decision Making & the Will of God*.

More "How To's"

When confronted with a specific situation in which they had not received any direct statement about a solution, the apostles and elders of the church in Jerusalem went through a decision-making process about how to help new Gentile believers. Their process included: (1) debating the issue, 15:7-12, (2) application of Scripture, 15:14-18, and (3) reaching a conclusion about what *"seemed good,"* 15:22,25,28.[1]

After considering the Scripture, Peter reached a conclusion. He expressed his opinion with the statement: *"Therefore it is my judgment that..."* (15:19). After they had debated all the relevant information, we read this conclusion in verse 25:

"It seemed good to us having become of one mind, to select men to send to you with our beloved Barnabas and Paul."

The apostles chose a solution to the problem that would strengthen the church and encourage the new believers that were being miss-led by false teachers from Judea.

Church leaders make similar decisions month after month. God has not chosen to give us the specific conclusion for every situation we must deal with in overseeing the local church, however the principles used by the apostles and elders in Jerusalem are the guidelines that will direct us to make wise decisions for church and home. These principles are:

1. Pray. Humbly ask God for wisdom.

2. Research the facts. Gather information from other believers who have had similar decisions to make in the past.[2]

3. Evaluate. Attach a value to your facts.

4. Decide. Make a choice that will be most honoring to God.

It is important for us to remember that God is *training* believers to be good decision makers. God works through Christian men and women by means of the wisdom, knowledge and understanding that we gain from the Scriptures. He expects us to make good decisions. Paul makes this clear when he says:

> *"...do you not know that the saints will judge the world? And if the world is judged by you, are you not competent to constitute the smallest law courts? Do you not know that we shall judge angels? How much more matters of this life."*

I Corinthians 6:1-3

I'd much rather receive advice from a Christian, who is knowledgable concerning God's Word that teaches how people ought to believe and live, than from someone who is unaware of that source of wisdom!

Scripture quotes on how "they" decided:
Ask the members of the study group to turn to these verses in their Bible (also list the references and briefly state the reasons in the margin of their workbook).

- "...we thought it <u>best</u>..." I Thessalonians 3:1-2

- "...I thought it <u>necessary</u>..." Philippians 2:25-26

- "...if it is <u>fitting</u>..." I Corinthians 16:3-4

- "...it is not <u>desirable</u>..." Acts 6:2-4

- "...in order that he might not have to spend time in Asia, <u>for he was hurrying</u> to be in Jerusalem..." Acts 20:16

- "...if any man aspires to the office of overseer, it is a fine work he <u>desires</u> to do." I Timothy 3:1

"You can't live a Christian life with no more than human resources."

Tony Evans

A <u>Plan</u> For Making Decisions

The value and importance of rules, whether they are God's or man's, can be seen by the contrasting popularity between American and Chinese baseball:

> **The American version of baseball** enjoys a great following, but the Chinese method of play has not been widely embraced. Although the games are played virtually the same way, there is one major exception.
>
> In Chinese baseball, the fielders can do anything they want once the ball leaves the pitcher's hand. They can move first base to the outfield if the batter is a slow runner. For heavy hitters, the entire team may move to the outfield. The bases can be moved into one pile, or further separated to get an easy out. In essence, once the baseball is pitched, anything can happen. Without a doubt, the lack of rules and order in Chinese baseball have prevented it from becoming a popular pastime like its American counterpart.
>
> In every arena of life we need rules, laws, and boundaries to foster well-being. Unfortunately, and to our own disadvantage, we frequently disregard the necessary guidelines when we have a decision to make.[12]

Our LORD created us with incredible ability to receive information, evaluate it and store it for future reference.

> **Every second, the human brain receives** more than a hundred million separate messages. This is done through one hundred billion nerve cells that form one hundred trillion separate connections, each capable of representing a single bit of information.
>
> If this were recorded on paper, the information would fill twenty million volumes.
>
> To use the entire storage capacity of the brain a person would have to learn something new every second for ten million years.[3]

Regarding this staggering information, Joseph Stowell correctly says, *"the real challenge is not **how much** of our brain we use, but **how** we use it."*

In the following paragraphs I am going to explain the four principles to follow in the process of making good decisions. These steps are all used in the decision-making process that the apostles went through in Acts 15. Let's take a brief look at each step.

#1—Pray
(Asking God for <u>wisdom</u>)

Bill Hybles advises, *"People who want to be successful enlist superior help."*[10] Football teams hire strength coaches. We get golf lessons from a "golf pro." Students break through learning barriers with the help of a tutor.[9] God has superior help available for us through prayer.

Because decisions are often made under pressure and stress, asking for wisdom is often the step in decision making that is overlooked or left till last. We are dependent beings. We must ask God for guidance, but God does not intend that guidance be a shortcut to escape making decisions.[8] God's purpose in decision making is to help us to become better people. We become more skillful by making decisions.

In his book *Making Life Work*, Bill Hybles writes about a word-association quiz that he read to his children, when they were small.

> **When my children were very young**, I used to read…the description of a person who worked in a particular profession, and the kids had to name the most important tool that person would use in his or her work. I'd read about a carpenter, and the kids would shout out hammer. I'd read about a dentist, and they'd mumble drill. For a surgeon, the word would be scalpel. For a drummer, drumstick. For a bricklayer, trowel. For a seamstress, needle. For an astronomer, telescope. For a referee, whistle. For a writer, pen.
>
> What was significant about each of these tools of the trade was that to the worker who used them, they were indispensable. Without a hammer the carpenter couldn't build a house. Without a scalpel the surgeon couldn't perform an operation. Without a telescope the astronomer couldn't see the stars.[10]

When it comes to making decisions, **prayer** is the indispensable tool. Without it we're left without wisdom to enable us to make the right decisions.

"Prayers can't be answered until they are prayed. The greatest tragedy of life is not unanswered prayer but unoffered prayer."

F.B. Meyer

Note

In Ephesians 6:13-18, Paul tells us that the whole armor of God is to be put on with prayer:

- *"Praying always with all prayer and supplication in the Spirit, and watching thereunto with all perseverance and supplication for all saints."*

Note

When God answers our prayer for wisdom, the answer could include:

- the ability to see a situation from God's perspective

- the recollection or discovery of relevant Bible passages that would reveal divine wisdom

- the ability to apply specific Biblical principles to the immediate situation

- the perspective needed to wait on the Lord.[14]

The members of your study group might want to contribute other possibilities. Provide time for those who wish to respond.

Ask everyone to make a list of these possibilities in the margin of their workbook.

Note

Have you ever seen a magician perform? With slight of hand he will make it appear that people rise up off the ground; are sawn in half or disappear into thin air.

A magician can get you focused on one thing while he does something else, and you think a miracle has happened! You say, "Wow! How did he do that!"

He tricked you. That's how he did it. He made things appear one way when actually they were another.[11]

(continued on next page)

"If any of you lacks wisdom, let him ask of God, who gives to all liberally and without reproach, and it will be given to him."

James 1:5

We can't develop a good track record in decision making with a deficiency in wisdom. It is encouraging to read in verse 5 that our God is not a miser who hoards up wisdom, but rather, He will give it bountifully to all who will ask for it in faith. He also will not criticize us for what we do not know.[13] He desires that we become more capable at making decisions, and He will supply the wisdom to do it.

As we pray for wisdom, I am sure that it would be wise to search the Scriptures for the wisdom that has already been written down. This brings us to the next step in making decisions:

#2—Research
(Gathering Information)

The search for truth is the primary concern when we are gathering data. Scripture itself is truth. It is profitable for teaching, for reproof, for correction, for training in righteousness. Only truth can make the necessary adjustments in our misunderstandings. Acting on information, that we have not verified as dependable, can get us into some pretty risky situations.

The photographer for a national magazine was assigned to shoot a great forest fire. He was told that a small plane would be waiting to take him over the fire.

He arrived at the airstrip just an hour before sundown.

Sure enough the Cessna was waiting. He jumped in with his equipment and shouted, "Let's Go!"

The pilot swung the plane into the wind and soon they were in the air. "Fly over the north side of the fire," said the photographer, "and make several low-level passes."

"Why?" asked the nervous pilot.

"Because I'm going to take pictures!" retorted the photographer, "I'm a photographer, and photographers take pictures."

After a long pause, the pilot replied, "You mean, you're not the instructor?"[4]

We must check out the data upon which we are making decisions. We must be sure that it is true. Truth is the foundation for thinking accurately.[5]

You'll need to do some outside research in making choices, when the subject is not covered directly or by principle in the Bible. List your data on a sheet of paper under assets and liabilities for each of your options.[15]

In addition to outside research, Gary Friesen describes how we should obtain advice from wise counselors:

> *One should seek out two kinds of counselors. Of those who possess deep* **spiritual insight**, *the question should be asked: "Are you aware of any Biblical principles that touch upon my decision?" To those who have gone through relevant* **personal experiences**, *the query should be: "When you went through a similar experience, did you gain any insights that would be of value to me?"*[16]

After determining the trustworthiness of your information, the next step is to determine which of the facts are more valuable in making your decision.

#3—Evaluate
(Arranging the information according to importance)

Organizing our data according to the value that we assign to each of the facts is the third step in making decisions. The things that we value most will influence our choices.

> **For example, if you value** *personal happiness and pleasure above all else, that assigned value would lead you to make a decision about abortion that would line up on the side of "pro-choice." However, if you value each person (even the unborn) as being made in God's image, then your decision about abortion would be guided in the direction of "pro-life."*[6]

(continued from previous page)

The world system works that way. They have a great way of speaking. They have a great line. We are tricked into thinking that the value system of this world is truth.

"Lead me in Thy truth and teach me, for Thou art the God of my salvation. For Thee I wait all the day."

Psalm 25:5

Christian Values

Ask your study group members to write the following list of values in the margin of their workbook:

- People above possessions
- Others above self
- Eternity above the present
- Righteousness above the temporary pleasures of sin
- God's will above my will
- Forgiveness above revenge
- Giving above receiving
- Children over careers
- Character above credentials
- Truth above falsehood
- Fact above feeling
- Commitment above comfort
- Christ above culture[7]

You might want to continue this list as you receive ideas from the study group.

"The judgments of the Lord are true...they are more desirable than gold, yes, than much fine gold; sweeter also than honey..."

Psalm 19:9-10

Note

It was the opinion of Solomon that the wisdom and understanding which come from the Scriptures are extremely valuable:

- *"How blessed is the man who finds wisdom, and the man who gains understanding. For its profit is better than the profit of silver, and its gain than fine gold. She is more precious than jewels; and nothing you desire compares with her."* Proverbs 3:13-15

Ask the study group members to turn to these verses and write them in the margin of their workbook. See also Proverbs 8:10-11,19; 16:16; 20:15

"Wisdom"

"The practical use of knowledge; how to act under certain circumstances of testing; good judgment"

Although we develop our values through a number of sources, including our family, friends, entertainment, teachers, heroes, and the news media, it is the moral value system that we learn from Scripture that will establish a thought process that will make the path of our life easier to travel.

> **"Trust in the LORD with all your heart, and do not lean on your own understanding. In all your ways acknowledge Him, and He will make your paths straight."**
>
> Proverbs 3:5-6

Placing value on the Word of God is seen in the New American Standard translation of Psalm 119:11.

> **"Thy Word I have treasured in my heart, that I may not sin against Thee."**

Ranking Biblical instruction as more valuable than all else was the mind set of the psalmist as he wrote:

> **"The law of Thy mouth is better to me than thousands of gold and silver."**
>
> Psalm 119:72

> **"Therefore I love Thy commandments above gold, yes, above fine gold."**
>
> Psalm 119:127

The next step of the thinking process involves discernment. Therefore, we must pray again for the ability to consider the available information and make a correct decision.

#4—Decide

(Making up your mind about the <u>best</u> choice)

If the information you have is true, and you have arranged these truths according to their importance based on your understanding of right and wrong, then the decision should be the easy part.[17]

If your decision involves a moral choice, then the choice must be righteous. If the choice is nonmoral, then the choice should be that which is most beneficial for Christ and our mission. In other words, which decision will work best to glorify and please God?

Remember that your choice involves a course of behavior. How we make up our mind will determine how we live. Or, as Joseph Stowell puts it:

> "Wrong values can lead to wrong conclusions, in spite of right information. And wrong conclusions result in wrong, unproductive, and even disastrous consequences."[18]

This shows the need to exercise the wisdom for which we prayed in the very first step to decision making. J. Vernon McGee defines wisdom as *the practical use of knowledge. It is to know **how** to act under certain circumstances of testing, of trial, or when problems or questions arise.*[21] The Webster's Dictionary defines wisdom as *good judgment.*

It is usually in times of trouble (trials or testing) that we feel forced to make decisions under the pressure of compelling influences. These difficulties that we face reveal our lack of wisdom in a particular area in which we must make a decision. When this deficiency of wisdom in a specific area becomes evident, then our prayer can become specifically focused on that special wisdom that we are lacking. It's about how to use the knowledge that we have gathered concerning the particular decision we must make.

So, we go to the Lord in prayer, asking for this specific wisdom because the Scripture teaches us that "...*the LORD gives wisdom,*" Proverbs 2:6.

To Whom Does God Give Wisdom?

(What else should we know about receiving wisdom?)

Wisdom is available to believers who possess certain character qualities. As we look at each characteristic, do a self-examination to see if you are among those who qualify. The people who will find wisdom have an understanding that:

#1—We do not <u>naturally</u> possess wisdom.

If we think that we or any other human being (including our close friends) have a better plan than God does about how our life ought to

Note

Some decisions such as those regarding moral compromise must be made ahead of time:

- The proper decision is to **avoid** sexual temptation.

If the decision is made well in advance (like right now) you can avoid having to try to make the decision in the midst of a sexually tempting situation.[19]

- *"Now then, my son, listen to me, and do not depart from the words of my mouth. Keep your way far from her, and do not go near the door of her house."* Proverbs 5:7-8

Make your decision now in broad daylight, while your thinking is clear and your mind is in control of your body.[20]

Activity

Ask the group to turn to Job 28:1-28 and read together the lengthy statement that Job makes regarding the location and source of wisdom. Point out how Job goes to great lengths to show that man cannot find wisdom down here on earth anywhere.

Illustration

J. Vernon McGee comments:

"When I am in Florida I always enjoy going to the home and laboratory of Thomas A Edison at Fort Myers. There is a museum there now. The thing that has always amazed me is his search for synthetic rubber. Firestone and Ford had their homes right next to Edison, and you can understand why they were interested in the project and were working with him. There were several hundred test tubes in his lab. Edison was taking everything that was imaginable and testing it to see if he could get synthetic rubber from it. Do you know that he found some of it in dandelions, of all things…As I stood in that laboratory and looked at those hundreds of test tubes and thought of the hours that he and his helpers had spent there, testing this and that and the other thing in order to try to find it, I thought, 'My, how little attention is given to the Word of God where one could do some real testing and some real study.'"[24]

The wisdom of God is worth our every effort to obtain.

be lived, we will need that attitude corrected before we are able to receive God's wisdom.

> **"Do not be wise in your own eyes; Fear the LORD and turn away from evil."**
>
> Proverbs 3:7

God's wisdom is not found here on this earth, and it cannot be obtained by human intelligence.

> **"But where can wisdom be found? And where is the place of understanding? Man does not know its value, nor is it found in the land of the living. The deep says, 'It is not in me', and the sea says, 'It is not with me.'"**
>
> Job 28:12-14

#2—God's wisdom is <u>extremely valuable</u> and worth our <u>every effort</u> to obtain.

Wisdom is given to those who become serious about pursuing it.

> **"If you seek her (wisdom) as silver, and search for her as for hidden treasure; then you will discern the fear of the LORD and discover the knowledge of God."**
>
> Proverbs 2:4-5

> **"I (wisdom) love those who love me; and those who diligently seek me will find me."**
>
> Proverbs 8:17

***Suppose you were informed** by a local mining company that there was a wide rich vein of gold running through your property just behind your house. After being advised that the gold was located approximately 50 feet below the surface, what measures would you take in order to reach the wealth that was available to you?*

The use of heavy expensive equipment would not be out of the question. You'd probably work long hours—even well into the night. You might hire others, with experience and skill, to help you in the mining venture. The quicker you reached the gold the better off you'd be. After all, what good is it going to be to you as long as it stays buried so far away?

The same serious pursuit is necessary is we qualify to receive the wisdom that is more valuable than silver and gold.

#3 <u>Humility</u> is the proper attitude of one who will receive wisdom.

The Bible says that a scoffer will not find wisdom (Proverbs 14:6), but one who is humble (distrustful of himself and fearing his own understanding, the abandonment of self-confidence and self-will)[22] will receive wisdom.

"When pride comes, then comes dishonor, but with the humble is wisdom."

Proverbs 11:2 NASV

"For it is written, 'I will destroy the wisdom of the wise, and the cleverness of the clever I will set aside.' Where is the wise man? Where is the scribe? Where is the debater of this age? Has not God made foolish the wisdom of the world?"

I Corinthians 1:19-20 NASV

#4—<u>Respect</u> is the proper attitude <u>toward God</u>, if one desires wisdom.

As we saw in Job's discussion of wisdom in Job 28:28, *"the fear of the LORD is wisdom…,"* the *"fear of the LORD"* is a respect for His authority and instruction.[23]

Imagine that you are *driving down a major interstate at a speed of 85 miles per hour in a 65 mph zone. You are in a hurry, but as you crest the hill, you see a highway patrol car stopped on the side of the highway with*

Illustration

The U.S. standard railroad gauge (distance between the rails) is four feet, eight-and-one-half inches. Why such an odd number? Because that's the way they built them in England, and American railroads were built by British expatriates.

Why did the English adopt that particular gauge? Because that's the width they built their tramways, and the tramways were built by the same standards that they used to build wagons.

Why were wagons built to that scale? So that the width of the wheels would match the ruts on the roads. So who built those old rutted roads?

The first long-distance highways in Europe were built by Imperial Rome for the benefit of their legions. The roads have been in use ever since. The ruts were first made for Roman war chariots. Four feet, eight-and-one-half inches was the width a chariot needed to be able to accommodate the rear ends of two war horses.[35]

Some lasting decisions are based on tradition rather than good reasoning.

"Buy the truth and do not sell it. Get wisdom and instruction and understanding."
Proverbs 23:23

Note

The contrast between the wisdom of the world and the wisdom that we are praying for is described in James 3:13-18:

• *"Who among you is wise and understanding? Let him show by his good behavior his deeds in the gentleness of wisdom. But if you have bitter jealousy and selfish ambition in your heart, do not be arrogant and so lie against the truth. This wisdom is not that which comes down from above, but is earthly, natural, demonic. For where jealousy is and selfish ambition exist, there is disorder and every evil thing. But the wisdom from above is first pure, then peaceable, gentle, reasonable, full of mercy and good fruits, unwavering, without hypocrisy. And the seed whose fruit is righteousness is sown in peace by those who make peace."*

its blue lights flashing. Suddenly, you take your foot off the accelerator pedal and return to the legal speed—That's a respect for the authority of the highway patrol.

That, to a small degree, is comparable to a respect for our Lord's authority. He has all authority in Heaven and earth. The fear of the LORD is the opposite of despising Him and it results in:

✦ *Hating evil, pride, arrogance, the evil way and a perverse mouth,* Proverbs 8:13

✦ *Walking uprightly and having strong confidence,* Proverbs 14:2, 26

✦ *Departing from evil,* Proverbs 16:6

✦ *Hope,* Proverbs 23:17-18

✦ *Praise,* Proverbs 31:30

#5—Hearing and accepting <u>reproof</u> and <u>discipline</u> is the path to wisdom.

Wisdom involves correcting our present understanding or behavior through instruction, both from the Scriptures as well as from a fellow believer.

"He whose ear listens to the life-giving reproof will dwell among the wise."

Proverbs 15:31 NASV

"Listen to counsel and accept discipline, that you may be wise the rest of your days."

Proverbs 19:20 NASV

#6—Living with <u>integrity</u> is the proper manner of life for one to receive wisdom.

When the LORD said that He would not withhold any good thing from those who walk uprightly (with integrity), that included wisdom.

"He stores up sound wisdom for the upright..."

Proverbs 2:7 NASV

#7—*The request for wisdom through prayer must be made with no <u>doubting</u>.*

Confidence in the Lord, about His willingness or ability to grant the request, is the necessary way to ask for wisdom. We can not come to God with uncertainty for that is an insult to Him.[25]

> **"But if any of you lack wisdom, let him ask of God, who gives to all men generously and without reproach, and it will be given to him. But let him ask in faith without any doubting, for the one who doubts is like the surf of the sea driven and tossed by the wind. For let not that man expect that he will receive anything from the Lord."**
>
> James 1:5-7 NASV

Wisdom is something that we can pray for someone else. Paul prayed for the Colossians this way.

> **"For this reason also, since the day we heard of it, we have not ceased to pray for you and to ask that you may be filled with the knowledge of His will in all spiritual wisdom and understanding."**
>
> Colossians 1:9 NASV

Paul seems to be saying here and in verse 10 that we can count on God to supply this wisdom as we gain knowledge about Him through reading and studying His Word. The trials that we face (the context of James) drive us to the Bible for answers. There in the Scriptures we find wisdom and apply that wisdom to our present circumstances.

Regarding our faith in times like this, Gary Friesen explains:

> **The single condition of unadulterated faith** *addresses the stance of the believer's heart in the face of trials. From the perspective of faith, the Christian realizes that God has neither abandoned him, nor turned against him—even though he has come upon hard times. Faith recognizes that the crucibles of life are divinely appointed, and seeks to cooperate with the Refiner's purpose. Faith does not reserve the right to reject God's wisdom*

"The fruit of the righteous is a tree of life, and he who is <u>wise</u> wins souls."

Proverbs 11:30

Note

The phrase *"make your paths straight"* means that God will make the course of your life smoother or more successful than it might have been. This is a major theme in the book of Proverbs.

- *"The righteousness of the blameless will smooth his way, but the wicked will fall by his own wickedness."* 11:5

The immediate context of Proverbs chapter 3 concerns the ways our life will experience a smoother path rather than a rough one.

- A longer and more peaceful life, 3:2-2
- Favor and good understanding, 3:3-4
- Healing and refreshment to your body, 3:7-8
- Your barns filled with plenty and your vats overflow with new wine, 3:9-10

Memory Verse
Proverbs 3:5-6

after it is given, but submits in advance to the higher ways and thoughts of the heavenly Father.[26]

We must be growing in our ability to make wise decisions.

Our choices and actions are continually observed by the unsaved world around us. Since we represent the only true and living God (as His ambassadors), our wisdom and understanding should be evident to everyone. We must redeem the time, for we do not know when our days here are over, and we will never again have a chance to lead others to the truth about Jesus Christ and His way of salvation.

The God of <u>Truth</u>
(Developing complete <u>confidence</u> in the Lord)

What we believe about the trustworthiness of God will effect every major decision we make. Now remember that faith in God has to do with our believing that what He has spoken is truth. It is *not faith* to trust the Lord to do something *that He has not said* He will do. But where He has spoken, He is as good as His Word!

> *"Trust in the LORD with all your heart, and do not lean on your own understanding. In all your ways acknowledge Him, and He will make your paths straight."*
>
> Proverbs 3:5-6 NASV

To "acknowledge God in all your ways" is to trust His judgment as it is expressed in His Word, instead of choosing your own ideas about success and happiness.[27] Confidence in the Lord is built as we learn through experience that He is all wise and ever faithful.

Bill Hybles addresses the personal dimension of trusting God in his book, *Making Life Work*. Although this is a rather lengthy segment , it offers some excellent insight as to how we can begin trusting the Lord one day at a time. Because there is no shortcut to trust, Hybles explains:

> *Perhaps it will help to imagine* a dating relationship you had in the past. Think back to a young man or woman who made your heart skip a beat. Can you remember the day you

first summoned the courage to ask that person for a date? or to accept a date?

During those first points of interaction, you were undoubtedly watching closely to see how trustworthy the new focus of your romantic interest was. Whether you were consciously testing that person or doing so on a subconscious level, you were fitting together the various components of what you saw in that person in order to determine whether or not this was someone you could really trust.

If he said he would be at your house at 7:00 p.m., you were a bit relieved when he showed up on time. Had he showed up an hour late without so much as a mention of his tardiness, you probably would have cringed, even if only on the inside. Punctuality may seem like a small thing, but deep inside you knew it was an indicator of a person's trustworthiness. How could you entrust the deeper issues of life to someone who wasn't even trustworthy enough to show up on time?

But let's assume your date showed up on time and proved trustworthy in regard to other relatively minor issues in life. The next step in developing trust was probably to take some conversational risks and discuss a few matters of the heart. As the other person spoke, you listened carefully, trying to discern the ring of truth in his or her words. Did this person's thoughts, ideas and descriptions of experiences seem grounded and believable, or did they sound farfetched and a bit untethered from reality?

And when you spoke honestly and openly, did that person listen carefully and respond appropriately? Did he or she offer good insights, heartfelt compassion, thoughtful affirmations or necessary challenges? The nature of that conversation and every conversation that followed either enhanced or eroded your trust in this person.

If your trust grew to the point where you decided to date this person exclusively, then the trust test continued on a higher level. It had to. The greater the commitment involved in a relationship, the greater the level of trust that is required. What

Note

Willingness to *"trust in the Lord with all of our heart"* for some people might be a great deal more difficult because of having been hurt in the past when we put our trust in someone who let us down or even caused great hurt.

The evil or inconsistent character of a significant person in our life can cause unbelievable disappointment.

Let me encourage you to consider that not everyone is a bad risk. There are some people that we can fully trust without any doubt.

Certainly our heavenly Father is completely trustworthy. Though others might prove to be a bad risk, our God *(the God of all truth)* will never betray our trust. His promises are not just words on a page. His faithfulness throughout all the ages has been documented. His goodness is never a disguise for other intentions.

We need never be suspicious of His character. There is no substantial reason to believe that the wisdom given by Him in the Scriptures is not reliable.

"Your love, O LORD, reaches to the heavens, your faithfulness to the skies." Psalm 36:5

What's your opinion on the truthfulness of Christ?

began as attention to your partner's punctuality and later as attention to his or her verbal trustworthiness has grown into a concern over issues like long-term loyalty, fidelity and dependability. As the commitments become broader and the disclosures deeper, the breadth and depth of trust must similarly increase. This is part of what it means to make life work in relationships. And we can't sit passively waiting for trust to grow. Building trust requires action. We need to take little steps and then assess the progress. We need to take little risks and then evaluate the consequences.

After engaging in that process for months, perhaps even years, we come to a point where we can say, "I can fully trust this person."[29]

Learning to trust someone involves taking a risk. It is "wiskey business" (as Elmer Fudd says). Perhaps if we could read a person's resume and letters of recommendation from others, who have known them for a good while, we would be more willing to confirm their truthfulness in an experience of our own.

We can be assured, however, that God has never broken a single promise. Joshua examined the record and found that:

> **"Not one of all the LORD'S good <u>promises</u> to the house of Israel failed; <u>every one was fulfilled</u>."**
>
> Joshua 21:45 NIV

In Solomon's prayer at the dedication of the house of the LORD, he said with a loud voice:

> **"Praise be to the LORD, who has given rest to His people Israel, just as He promised. <u>Not one word has failed of all the good promise</u>, which He gave through His servant Moses."**
>
> I Kings 8:56 NIV

After his prayer of dedication was over, Solomon then appealed to his people to:

"Let your heart therefore be wholly devoted to the LORD our God, to walk in His statutes and to keep His commandments, as at this day."

I Kings 8:61 NASV

My challenge to you is similar: *"Trust in the LORD with all your heart and lean not to your own understanding. In all your ways acknowledge Him and He will make your paths straight."* You can trust Him with every detail of your life. He is completely committed to fulfilling His promises. He is always dependable.

PRAYER:

"Lord, I am willing to trust You with my whole heart. I am refusing to rely on my own understanding of things. I will acknowledge You in each decision, because I value the wisdom from Your holy Word. Amen."

HANDLING THE TOUGH TIMES

Trials Are Designed To <u>Strengthen</u> Your <u>Faith</u>

*W*hen *iron ore is dug out* of a mountain, it is worth only a few dollars per ton. But when that same ore is placed in a furnace and put under enormous heat and pressure, it is changed into a high grade of steel.[1]

Tough times in our life are used to build our saving faith into a much stronger, persevering confidence in God and His Word. God does not send us through trials to see if we *have* faith, but rather, He sends our *saving faith* through a process that will make it more durable. In the midst of our trial, God will identify our weaknesses in order to temper our faith and make us strong in that area where we were once weak. Adversity refines us into the strong people He has planned for us to become. He can't use us if we are weak.

God is developing you. He is bringing you to the point to where your faith stands the test, no matter how hot the fire gets.[3]

It is good to know from the very beginning of this study that the trials (troubles) we face are designed for a limited time. It is so easy to think that the trouble that we are presently facing will go on for ever. While some circumstances continue longer than others, most of our tough times change very quickly. Peter explains :

"After you have suffered for a little while, the God of all grace, who called you to His eternal glory in Christ, will Himself, perfect, confirm, strengthen, and establish you."

I Peter 5:10 NASV

In *A View from the Zoo*, Gary Richmond tells about the birth of a giraffe:

The first thing to emerge are the baby giraffe's front hooves and head. A few minutes later the plucky newborn is hurled forth, falls ten feet, and lands on its back. Within seconds, he rolls to an upright position with his legs tucked under his body. From this position he considers the world for the first time and shakes off the last vestiges of the birthing fluid from his eyes and ears.

The mother giraffe lowers her head long enough to take a quick look. Then she positions herself directly over her calf. She waits for about a minute, and then she does the most unreasonable thing. She swings her long, pendulous leg outward and kicks her baby, so that it is sent sprawling head over heals.

When it doesn't get up, the violent process is repeated over and over again. The struggle to rise is momentous. As the baby calf grows tired, the mother kicks it again to stimulate its efforts... Finally, the calf stands for the first time on its wobbly legs.

Then the mother giraffe does the most remarkable thing. She kicks it off its feet again. **Why?** *She* *wants it to remember how it got up. In the wild, baby giraffes must be able to get up quickly in order to stay with the herd, where there is safety. Lions, hyenas, leopards, and wild hunting dogs all enjoy young giraffes, and they'd get it too, if the mother didn't teach her calf to get up quickly and get with it…*[4]

Can you see the parallel in your own life? Have there been times when you just stood up after a trial, only to be knocked down again by the next. God wants you to remember how it was that you got up (how you made a good decision in daily life).

Oh, by the way, the context of our verse in I Peter 5:10 is all about the devil stalking **us** <u>like a lion</u>, so, we must learn the same thing.

> **"Be of sober spirit, be on the alert. Your adversary, the devil, prowls about like a roaring lion, seeking someone to devour. But resist him, firm in your faith, knowing that the same experiences of suffering are being accomplished by your brethren who are in the world. And after you have suffered for a little while, the God of all grace, who called you to His eternal glory in Christ, will Himself, perfect, confirm, strengthen and establish you. To Him be dominion forever and ever. Amen."**

I Peter 5:8-10 NASV

Like the young giraffe needed to **practice** getting up as quickly as possible in order to stay with the herd, God has planned that you and I should go through practice of a different kind. Our practice is <u>to become skilled at making good decisions and following through with appropriate actions</u>.

"Practice" means to take the truth that we are learning and use it in real life situations. You have to be alert to grasp this one. When we learn something from the Bible (like how to make good choices), we will very soon run right into some kind of trouble that we hadn't planned on. When that happens, we are prone to think, *"What in the world is going on? Why is God letting this happen to me?"* He's letting it happen to you to give you practice.[5]

"There is nothing, no circumstances, no trouble, no testing, that can ever touch me until, first of all, it has gone past God…right through to me. If it has come that far, it has come with great purpose, which I may not understand at the moment; but I refuse to become panicky, as I lift my eyes to Him and accept it as coming from the throne of God for some great purpose of blessing to my own heart; no sorrow will ever disturb me, no trial will ever alarm me, no circumstance will cause me to fret, for I shall rest in the joy of what my Lord is. This is the rest of victory."

Alan Redpath,
Victorious Christian Living

Note

During the time of Israel's captivity in Babylon, God encouraged the captives of Israel, through Jeremiah with these words:

- *"For I know the plans that I have for you, declares the LORD, plans for welfare and not for calamity to give you a future and a hope."* Jeremiah 29:11

"Practice"

"Means to take the truth you've learned and use it in real life situations"

The wilderness was a practice field for the nation of Israel:

"And you shall remember all the ways the LORD God has led you in the wilderness these 40 years, that He might humble you, testing you to know what was in your heart, whether you would keep His commandments or not..."

Deut. 8:2-3 NASV

Illustration

Toddlers and crawlers make bad choices, therefore we have to put clips on cabinet doors and pottie seats, gates on stairways, safety belts on high chairs, rat poison up out of their reach, and keep them out of mud puddles.

They'll even drink detergent. They do these things because they haven't had time to learn truth and practice it.

(continued on next page)

Any good sports team has a room with a "chalk board" where the coaching staff teaches the fundamentals of the game. Once you've learned the basics, they send you out to the **practice field** where you get experience using what you learned on the "chalkboard."

We become stronger and more skilled as we learn the truth and God provides the opportunity to use it. We must not forget how we made those good decisions. It's the safe thing to do. He teaches us truth and then gives us responsibility. If He only teaches us without sending us through some trials, then we're not going to develop.

Tony Evans gives a perfect example with the truth we learn about "love" (agape)—The truth is: love is not a feeling, but rather a decision of the will to do for the one loved what's best for them, even at your own expense.

> *You say, "**Wow! That's news. I always thought love was a <u>feeling</u>. Praise God that I've learned the real meaning of love!**" And as soon as you get in the car, God puts you on the practice field of life! Somebody treats you very unkindly, and you have a fit! "**How dare they treat me like that!**" You don't understand that God is giving you practice... Once you learn the truth, God is going to create for you a "gymnasium experience." It's like the practice field. He's going to put you in a work-out-room. He's going to give you some weights, and He's going to say, "**Lift this. I've shown you what weights and plates and dumbbells are, now I am going to put the weight on your shoulders. You're in the gymnasium of life. Let Me see if you've learned how to lift**."*
>
> *Now, when you are in the "gym" you're not suppose to ask the question: "**What am I doing in the gym?!**" What you're suppose to do in the gym is to pump iron! The "gymnasium" is a circumstance in life and what you are suppose to do is remember the truth you've learned and practice it.*[6]

When we get the Biblical principles and apply them in practice, we become stronger in Christian character and discernment. The truth that we have practiced becomes a part of who we are.

Then what about the people who don't learn the Biblical principles about how to live? The truth is that we are going to face trials whether we have those Biblical principles or not. When we face the tough times of life, without the necessary truth to handle them skillfully, then we become angry. We begin to think that God is not fair. These immature Christians make bad decisions because they either haven't had *time* to practice or they do not *care* to practice.

> **But I thought** *that I am now a "new person and that old things have passed away." Doesn't that mean that I should not have to go through these trials or have to <u>practice</u> in order to live skillfully? Isn't it true that my bad choices are a thing of the past? And since "all things have become new," isn't my past tendency to make selfish decisions replaced by a new consistency in making godly choices?[6]*

The thought that once a person becomes a Christian, he or she no longer experiences the element of foolishness in making life decisions and that all thoughts of lust or hatred are forever gone from our mind comes from an *incorrect* understanding of a very special verse.

> **"Therefore if any man <u>be</u> in Christ, <u>he is</u> a new creation: old things have passed away; behold, all things are become new."**

II Corinthians 5:17 KJV

Actually the meaning of this is:

> **"Therefore if any man <u>be</u> in Christ, <u>there is</u> a new creation…"**

The meaning of Paul's writing in this chapter is that when a person becomes a Christian he finds himself in a whole new world (creation). It is his <u>environment</u> that has the radical change, not his <u>character</u>. The *New Geneva Study Bible* shows that this is the proper understanding. Here's what Paul is telling us:

"old things have passed away"

- ✦ Transferred from the kingdom of darkness to the kingdom of light. Ephesians 5:8-11; Colossians 1:13; I Thessalonians 5:4-11

- ✦ No longer dead in sins. Ephesians 2:1

- ✦ Not a condemned person. John 3:18

(continued from previous page)

But because of practice, mature adults will say: "Detergent is for dishes; rat poison is for rats; that person is not someone that I should hang around with; that's not an occupation I should get into." And you won't step in the same mud puddle every day.[7]

"Ellipsis"

Notice that *"be"* and *"he is"* are in italics. This means that they are not in the Greek writing of this verse. The literary term for this is Ellipsis. This means that some of the material is left out because it is to be understood by the reader, in light of the topic of conversation.

It's the same in our language. If you ask, *"Where did the plane go?"*

And I say, *"Down."* You clearly understand that *"Down"* means *"The plane went down."*

Some of the Corinthian believers were not good ambassadors for Christ. Their life was characterized by immorality, strife, jealousy, divisions, getting drunk and taking one another to court. Yet in the same context of rebuking them, Paul used the reminder that the Holy Spirit was in them as the motivation to change the way they were living, I Corinthians 3:1-3; 6:1-20; 11:20-32.

Activity

Ask the members to bring to mind a particular Christian friend, and think, for a few moments about that person's character. Then ask them to make a list of three things that they would change (if they could) about that person's life.

They might also make a list of the three things that they were well satisfied with about their own character, and then make a list of the three things that they need to ask God to help them change about their character during these next days and weeks.

The truth is: All of us have areas of our life that still need fixing.

All of our old (bad) ways are not gone away.

"all things have become new"

✦ Citizens of another world. II Corinthians 5:20; Philippians 3:20

✦ Ambassadors for our new King. II Corinthians 5:20

✦ We have a new Father, God. John 1:12; Romans 8:15; I John 3:2

We live in a *new world* with a different kingship, citizenship and eternal destiny.[8] Paul is telling us that when we become believers, a *whole new creation* opens up before our eyes. We see for the first time that:

> *"...all things are of God, who has reconciled us to Himself by Jesus Christ, and has given to us the ministry of reconciliation."*

> II Corinthians 5:18 NIV

The incentive to develop godly character by practicing truth as we face trouble in this world is our new life as a citizen of Heaven and as a new ambassador for the King of the universe.

But Why Use Trouble To Train Us?

If God didn't allow us to get into tough situations, we would never turn to Him for the wisdom and knowledge that we need for maturity.

Imagine that we are walking through the large shopping mall in the town where you live. You notice about thirty yards in front of you that there is a man holding up a bright orange life vest. As you draw near you realize that he is telling the shoppers, as they walk by, the important facts about the life vest: how much weight it will support in the water, how it is so easy to use, etc. But no one is stopping to hear the sales pitch, though the man is doing a very professional job of representing his life-saving product. Even you choose to keep walking. You are thinking about too many other things that are more important right now.

Now imagine that you are on a cruise in the North Pacific and that the hull of your ship has just been pierced by an iceberg.

You are once again in a hurry as you walk quickly with a great *number of other people to the front of the ship. As you make your way in the crowd, you notice the same man holding the same bright orange life vest. But this time every one is glued to every word as he explains the efficiency and use of the life-saving equipment.*[9]

What made the big difference? Why were people, who were at one time totally indifferent to the information about this bright orange vest, now so attached to his speech? What has changed? A life jacket can seem unnecessary until your ship begins to sink.[9]

Things We Need To Know <u>Before</u> Trouble Comes

The things we are about to learn will seem a whole lot more important some day when God allows us to face trials that threaten to sink our ship, but finding out how to survive must come before the trial.

Trials are inevitable.

"...<u>when</u> you encounter various trials."

James 1:1 NASV

It is a matter of "when" not "if" you encounter trials. We are appointed for this method of training.

"...and we sent Timothy, our brother and God's fellow worker, in the gospel of Christ, to strengthen and encourage you as to your faith; that no man may be disturbed by these afflictions; for you yourselves know that <u>we have been destined for this</u>."

I Thessalonians 3:3 NASV

Trials come in many varieties.

"...when you encounter <u>various</u> trials."

The trials of life come in many varieties, because God wants us to become mature and responsible in many areas of life.

Note

Trials, for the most part, are unannounced. The phrase *"fall into"* or *"encounter"* in James 1:2 is the same phrase that is used in Luke 10:30 where Jesus is explaining, *"...a certain man was going down from Jerusalem to Jericho; and he fell among robbers..."*

It's a term that refers to being suddenly engulfed in an unannounced landslide. You're OK on Monday but Tuesday you're hit by an unexpected crisis.[12] So, Christians can determine ahead of time to not be upset just because we didn't see the trial coming.

Activity

I once read about a man who, shortly before World War II, believed that a global conflict was coming.

He decided to find a place he could be safe whatever happened. He studied the map of the world and chose one of the most remote and least populated islands on the globe. He moved there. The island turned out to be Guadalcanal, the scene of one of the bloodiest battles in human history.[20]

Trials are inevitable. They will happen, no matter where we live. There are no short cuts.

Note

The term *"various"* means *"many faceted or many aspects."* This term is also used to describe the grace and wisdom of God:

- *"the manifold grace of God"* I Peter 4:10

- *"the manifold wisdom of God"* Ephesians 3:10

Our complexity of trials is overpowered by the grace and wisdom of God.[13]

"Consider"

"An accounting term that means to regard; to make a mental note; to record something in a ledger"

✦ Some trials involve the physical part of our life. You might receive a discouraging or frightening diagnosis from your physician. You not only feel pain, fear, and inconvenience, but you face a life that is possibly changed forever, bringing with it the changing of all of your plans and dreams. Perhaps this physical trial has come to someone else who is dear to you, and maybe it involves death and therefore tremendous loss.

✦ A trial can also be something that is heavy and troubling to your heart and can cause discouragement. This could be caused by a child who is disrespectful and disobedient or a spouse who doesn't understand or doesn't care. Maybe you have lost your job, or raise or promotion, and as far as you can see, you'll suffer severe financial difficulties. Money that you had counted on is now not available to pay your bills.

Trials can also come because of our representing Christ and His Word. Jesus tells us that when these things happen, we shouldn't be surprised, because, "*...in the world you will have tribulation...*" John 16:33.

> *"Beloved, <u>do not think it strange</u> concerning the fiery trial which is to try you, as though some strange thing has happened to you; but rejoice to the extent that you partake of Christ's sufferings, that when His glory is revealed you may also be glad with exceeding joy."*

> I Peter 4:12 KJV

Trials require us to <u>think</u>.

> *"<u>Consider</u> it all joy, my brethren, when you encounter various trials."*

> James 1:1 NASV

The word "consider" is a word used in the accounting profession.[10] It means to regard; to make a mental note; to record something on a ledger. It has nothing to do with how we feel, but how we *think*.[11] The most important time in our life to think is when we are encountering trouble.

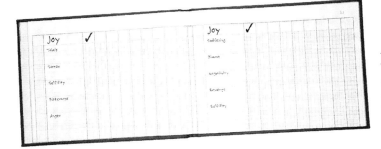

An accountant has a wide variety of columns in his ledger in which he could make an entry, just as we have numerous headings under which to record our experience during a trial. As the accountant would use a pencil to make an entry, believers are to mentally make a check mark in our mental ledger.

If our evaluation is done on the basis of our feelings, our mental notes would go down in the columns of Bitterness, Resentment, Revenge, Self-pity, Blame or a great variety of incorrect evaluations. Kinda' like, *"What am I doing in the gym?!"*

But, if we wisely use the first moments of a trial to <u>think what trials are all about</u>, we would evaluate the trial as an opportunity of a life time to allow God to make us more like Christ. In a time of crisis or sorrow, God is setting us up to be heroes (the ones who really come through in a time when others need to be rescued).

"But how can I be a hero?"

You see, a trial most often involves two or more people. It is usually some kind of relational thing: marriage difficulties or parenting problems; conflict between friends or employer/employee disagreement. Bill Donahue would describe such opportunities as, ***"a place where truth meets life."*** He would call this a ***"moment."***[19] That's a time and place where the power of God is at work in our life. He is leading us to a *decision* and a *response* to His leadership. And when you seize the moment, you win the day. Others are influenced and often impressed. "Poof," you're a hero. You've decided that you will no longer endure trials without experiencing transformation. There are people out there who need to be rescued.

> ***During the Olympic Games*** *in Mexico City, in 1968, an hour after the winner of the Olympic marathon had already crossed the finish line, John Stephen Akwari of Tanzania entered the far end of the stadium. The lone runner pressed on in pain, hobbling every step, his leg bloody and bandaged, to cross the finish line as the small crowd roared out its appreciation. Afterward, a reporter asked the runner why he had not retired from the race, since he*

Note

Trials are not a joyous experience. As a matter of fact, they are often quite distressing.

- *"In this you greatly rejoice, even though now for a little while, if necessary, you have been **distressed** by various trials."* I Peter 1:6

"And God is able to make all grace abound to you, that always having all sufficiency in everything, you may have an abundance for every good deed." II Corinthinans 9:8

Material

Consider having a ledger book to display for the study group.

When tough times hit, what's your attitude?

Discussion

Ask the members of the study group if they can recall a time when they came through in a game or a crisis.

It's OK to share some good things that you have accomplished during a tough time both on the court and off.

"Men occasionally stumble over the truth, but most pick themselves up and hurry off as if nothing had happened."

Winston Churchill

had no chance of winning. He seemed confused by the question. Finally he answered, "My country did not send me to Mexico City to start the race. They sent me to finish."[18]

When God allows another trial to come into our life, it's more important than the Olympics! Do we just put on the track uniform and go through the first few miles, or do we finish the race? Stay with Him when you want to quit!

Understanding that **"...no one should be shaken by these afflictions; for we our selves know that we have been destined for this."** With that truth in mind, we can make an entry in the column marked **"Joy."** During a crisis, you won't feel joy. You might even make the mark with tears in your eyes, but when we think clearly and correctly, we are now prepared to handle the trouble more skillfully. This is the way we must think every time a trial comes our way—like a powerful defensive team takes a goal-line stand to protect their lead in the fourth quarter, or one who hits a home run in the bottom of the ninth, to come from behind and win the game.

The big reason for joy.

The primary reason for joy is based upon what we know it will produce in our character. So, our thinking should be focused on what James says that we can **"know."**

> **"knowing that the testing of your faith produces endurance."**
>
> James 1:3 NASV

It is this certain knowledge in verse 3 that we can count on that is the basis for the joy mentioned in verse 2. We are promised that, if we allow it to do so, the trial that we are in, will work to achieve a resilient stability in our life. This knowledge does not produce a fun time but rather a deep joy of a reality that will be achieved. Just as we willingly swallow bad-tasting-medicine because we are aware of the health-giving results, we choose to consider the trial to be a positive thing in our life because of what it is producing.

> **We willingly swallow bad-tasting medicine, because we are aware of the life-giving results.**

In the motion picture Hook, *the once adventurous character, Peter Pan, had grown up. As the movie began, Peter was happily married and was the father of two children. But Captain Hook, always after revenge, kidnapped Peter's son and daughter. Hook held the children hostage and promised that they would never return unless Peter fought him once more in hand-to-hand combat.*

The problem now facing Peter is that, while at one time he was able to defeat Hook with his quickness and his ability to fly, he is now much older, and heavier, and can no longer fly. He seems to be in an impossible situation. His skill in flying was based on his ability to think happy thoughts. Now with his children in the hands of a murderous pirate and with his inability to rescue them, how could he think of anything happy?

Then Peter remembered his reason for wanting to grow up—a truth that changed Peter's whole out look on his situation. He wanted to grow up so he could be a dad. **"I'm a dad!"**

What ever else was wrong in his life at that moment, faded into the background compared to the deep joy of knowing that he was the father to two wonderful children. That knowledge brought the joy that enabled him to fly!—and everyone in the theater knew at that moment that Hook was in for a bad time!

"The question to be asked at the end of an educational step is not, 'What has the student learned?' but 'What has the student become?'"

United States President James Monroe

Dads understand that deep joy, but I think you will agree with me that moms know and understand an even deeper joy that is intimately associated with pain. Think about a mother in labor. There's plenty of pain. The contractions hurt more than words can express, but there is joy in the pain because of the knowledge that she will soon receive the child that she has waited and worked for all those months.

That's the kind of joy that is produced by knowing and looking forward to the end result of our trials. Jesus, **"...for the joy that was set before Him endured the cross..."** It was the joy of resurrection not the joy of crucifixion. He was joyful about Sunday morning, not Friday morning.[21]

Now let's summarize on a chart what we have covered so far.

It is one thing to know that, in Joshua's day, because of the power of the Almighty God:

- *"...the sun stood still in the midst of heaven, and hasted not to go down about a whole day."* Joshua 10:13

But it is another thing entirely to look with confidence to the One who is capable of doing mighty things in our behalf, because:

- *"...this God is our God for ever and ever..."* Psalm 48:14

It is stated again, in the New Testament, this way:

- *"Now to Him who is able to do exceeding abundantly beyond all that we ask or think, according to the power that works within us."* Ephesians 3:20

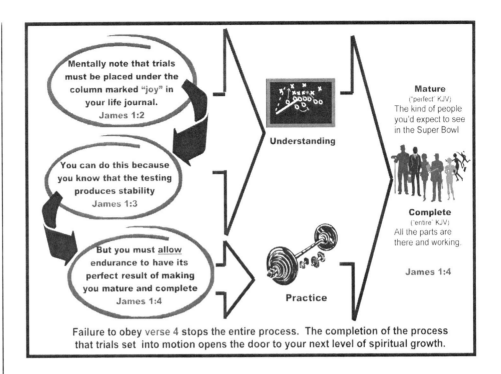

Mentally note that trials must be placed under the column marked "joy" in your life journal.
James 1:2

You can do this because you know that the testing produces stability
James 1:3

But you must <u>allow</u> endurance to have its perfect result of making you mature and complete
James 1:4

Understanding

Practice

Mature
("perfect" KJV)
The kind of people you'd expect to see in the Super Bowl

Complete
("entire" KJV)
All the parts are there and working.

James 1:4

Failure to obey verse 4 stops the entire process. The completion of the process that trials set into motion opens the door to your next level of spiritual growth.

Trials are testing our <u>faith</u> in God and His Word.

Although there are great varieties of trials that we will experience, every one of those trials is designed to **test your faith** in some special area in which you need more endurance.

> **"Knowing that the testing of your faith produces endurance."**

> James 1:3 NASV

In effect, God is saying, *"**Do you believe** that My Word is telling the truth when it says that I am a loving, merciful God, who causes all things to work out for good to those who love Me, to those who are called according to My purpose?* **Will you still <u>believe</u> that My Word is true when you experience trials that in no way seem fair, and it appears that I am not in control?"**

Our response to the test tells us how we are relating to God's Word. During trials we find out if we are continuing to rely on our old human view point to bring us through or if we have confidence enough in what God says to put His guidelines to work in our present situation. We find out if we are still going it on our own or if we are becoming quick to call on God in prayer in order to receive the skill to handle the situation wisely and the grace to remain steadfast during the ordeal.

Your faith in God and His Word is what must under go the tests of the many areas of life in order to strengthen your confidence in the integrity of His ideas over our human view point.[16] Trials reveal areas in our life that need to be changed.

Another fact that will encourage us as we endure the learning process of trials is that our kind and merciful God is in charge.

God is keeping a <u>careful watch</u> over the process.

There's a good deal of information about each trial that we do not know. When we first encounter a difficult situation, we are in the dark about a lot of the details. It is only by trusting our kind and wise God to handle the process, that we can turn a negative event into a positive one.

> *To develop a picture, a photographer begins with a negative, takes it into a darkroom, and at the proper moment shines light onto it. If the light is applied too early, the picture is ruined.*
>
> *In the darkroom of life experiences, God's timing is perfect and is applied in our lives at the proper moment to produce a beautiful picture of Himself.[14]*

Our Almighty God will faithfully control the amount of time that you will have to endure in the dark room of each trial. Peter confirms that our God has the ability to accomplish this.

> **"...the Lord knows how to rescue the godly from trials..."**
>
> II Peter 2:9 NIV

Paul explains that this very thing happened to him. As he tells Timothy about the persecutions and sufferings that he incurred in Antioch, Iconium and Lystra, Paul explains this incredible truth:

> **"...out of them all the Lord delivered me!"**
>
> II Timothy 3:11 NASV

King David said that it will work the same way for everyone who is living righteously while they are going through trials:

Note

When Lloyd C. Douglas, author of *The Robe* and other novels, was a university student. He lived in a boarding house. Downstairs on the first floor was an elderly, retired music teacher, now infirmed and unable to leave the apartment.

Douglas said that every morning they had a ritual they would go through together. He would come down the steps, open the old man's door, and ask, *"Well, what's the good news?"*

The old man would pick up his tuning fork, tap it on the side of his wheelchair, and say, *"That's Middle C! It was Middle C yesterday; it will be Middle C tomorrow; it will be Middle C a thousand years from now. The tenor upstairs sings flat, the piano across the hall is out of tune, but my friend, that is Middle C!"*

The old man had discovered one thing upon which he could depend, one constant reality in his life, one "still point in a turning world." For Christians, the one "still Point in a turning world" is Jesus Christ our Lord.[17]

"Jesus Christ is the same yesterday and today, yes and forever." Hebrews 13:8

Note

Since a number of our guidelines about trials have come from the book of James, it will be helpful to look at the following lists, which show James' purpose in writing his book as compared to Paul's purpose in writing the book of Romans.

Ask the members of the study group to fill in the missing words, as you go over the differences.

1. **Romans** is written to explain how a person is made <u>right</u> with God (that's faith without works).

   James is written to explain how a person, who has already been made right with God, is suppose to <u>live out his new life</u> in Christ (that is faith plus works).

2. **Romans** speaks about sinners becoming saints (faith without works).

   James talks about saints living saintly (faith plus works).

3. **Romans** tells how to go from earth to Heaven (faith without works).

   James tells how to live heavenly on earth (faith plus works).

(continued on next page)

"Many are the afflictions of the righteous; But the LORD delivers him out of them all."

Psalm 34:19 NASV

God knows exactly when and how He will rescue us from every situation, and He places us only in those situations that are bearable by human beings. He does not use angel-type trials for the purpose of strengthening the endurance of believers. We can be sure that He will lead us in and out of the troubles that we experience.

"No temptation has overtaken you but such as is common to man; and God is faithful, who will not allow you to be tempted beyond what you are able, but with the temptation will provide the way of escape also, that you may be able to endure it."

I Corinthians 10:13 NASV

God does not design or allow trials that will crush or break our will. He wants to change our understanding and give us wisdom through trials so that we will choose to submit our will to His divine purpose.

As we begin to understand the wisdom of God's principles, His commandments make sense to us. They seem very reasonable and good. We now have more confidence in Him and less confidence in the world's flawed way of reasoning.

In the Manhattan Project, scientists figured out how to unleash the power of the atom. It was an event that would change the course of history. This discovery ended the Second World War and now powers cities and submarines. From the secular standpoint, nuclear energy is the greatest power in the universe.

However, we have the real truth about power. It belongs to our great God.

"Ah Lord God! Behold, Thou hast made the heavens and the earth by Thy great power and by Thy outstretched arm! Nothing is too difficult for Thee."

Jeremiah 32:17 NASV

Trials drive us to *prayer*.

Once we have received the instructions about trials in James 1:1-4, we must make our request for wisdom, which is the skill to be used in the application of truth that we have just learned. *"How do we fly this thing?"* We are asking the great and mighty God for the skill to operate in the way prescribed in verses 1-4, when we encounter those "moments" that are designed to develop us into heroes.

> **"But if any of you lacks wisdom, let him ask of God, who gives to all men generously and without reproach, and it will be given to him."**
>
> James 1:5 NASV

By using the word "if," James assumes that everyone can admit this lack of wisdom, so by all means, ask—every time a trial comes into your path! Remember, all trials are different in some way, so we need to ask often. God will never rebuke us for admitting our lack of skill in the application of truth to our real life situations.

> *Several years ago, the evening news showed* police pursuing a government employee, who was driving a stolen U.S. Army tank. At speeds of forty to fifty miles per hour, he raced through inner-city streets, flattening cars, terrifying pedestrians, smashing into buildings, and toppling traffic signs. Finally, while trying to cross a major highway, he got hung up on the median wall. Police surrounded the tank and apprehended the suspect. The police worked hard to catch him because the stakes were high and the situation was urgent.[23]

What would it be like if we pursued wisdom with the same urgency and attention? How would our maturity level increase, if we got serious about the skill to navigate through trials in a way that brought about the completeness that Jesus Christ wants to build into our lives? As we respond to God's program to strengthen our faith, we model the Christian life for others who are looking for a leader.

****

The source of the trials that we have been studying is **external** (James 1:1-12). They are pressures that are allowed or brought about by God.

(continued from previous page)

4. **Romans** is about how to be justified (faith without works).

   James is about how to live like you are justified (faith plus works).

The theme of James is how believers can live godly lives while going through trials.

Note

Remember that when a writer in the New Testament uses the phrase *"My brethren,"* it limits his audience. This shows that he is writing to those who have already become Christians. So, the things that James is talking about in this context are relevant to the life of all **believers**.

Also see 1:16,18,19; 2:1,5,14; 3:1,10,12; 4:11; 5:7,9,10,12,19.

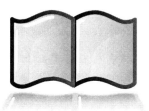

Memory Verse
II Peter 2:9

"Temptation"

"An enticement to disobey God's commandments by taking our God-given desires beyond God-given boundaries"

This would be contrary to the character of God

His intention is to strengthen us and produce stability in our life which will make us mature and complete.

There is another kind of pressure that gives us a great deal of trouble. The source of these bad times is **internal**. (James 1:13-17)

Temptation
(Pressure _We_ Bring On _Ourselves_)

Not only will we face trials in our daily life, we will also encounter temptations that are brought about by our own desires. It is pressure that comes, when we want to take our God-given desires beyond God-given boundaries.[22] Charles Stanley defines temptation as "an enticement to disobey God's commandments."[23]

> **For example, God has created within us** *a desire to have sexual involvement, and He has stated that our gratification of this desire must be within the limitation of marriage. It is when we experience the temptation to fulfill this desire outside the boundary of our marriage relationship that we are facing a decision about sin.*

James says that these temptations have nothing to do with God. He allows and sometimes sends trials, but we are responsible for temptations.

> **"Let no one say when he is tempted, 'I am being tempted by God;' for God cannot be tempted by evil, and He Himself does not tempt anyone."**
>
> James 1:13 NASV

It is not God's character to tempt anyone. We cannot blame Him for the regular struggle we have to move contrary to the commands, principles, and examples presented in the Scriptures. God does not place enticing situations before us that would cause us to sin.

It is not a sin to be tempted. It is however a sin when we *yield* to the temptation in violation of Biblical truth.

Sin doesn't _just happen_.

We will never come to the point in our spiritual maturity where we can <u>resist temptation</u> without being very prayerful and cautious. So don't treat temptation like it's no big thing. We must quickly remove ourselves from the circumstances that are enticing us to sin.

> *"Do not enter the path of the wicked, and do not proceed in the way of evil men. Avoid it, do not pass by it; turn away from it and pass on."*
>
> Proverbs 4:14-15 NASV

It is people who encourage us to make wrong choices in these situations. Often these people, who tempt us to sin are our "friends."

> *"My son, if sinners entice you do not consent."*
>
> Proverbs 1:10 NASV

Once we make the choice to give in to the enticement, that becomes sin. Temptation combined with the wrong decision produces sin.

Continued sin brings <u>physical death</u>.

The consequences of a life of sin is premature physical death, and it is the *"beloved brethren"* who are being warned about this deadly consequence. If sin is pursued by a believer, you will die before your time. No matter how old you are, your time could be running out. God could take you home early.

> *"Then when lust has conceived it gives birth to sin; and when sin is accomplished, it brings forth <u>death</u>. Do not be deceived my beloved brethren."*
>
> James 1:15-16 NASV

This important truth is woven all through Scripture. Paul says in Romans 8:6 that to be carnally minded is death, but to be spiritually minded is life and peace.

Note

Satan has designed this world system to appeal to our desires. TV and magazine advertisements and the movies are all crafted to stimulate our desire to be:

• Attractive

• Trim or thin

• Powerful

• Rich

• Accepted

They entice us to have:

• Automobiles

• Food

• Beer

• Hair

• Clothes

• Relief from pain

The opportunities available in politics, sports, and entertainment draw out the desires to be:

• Applauded

• Cheered

• Followed

• Obeyed

• Worshiped

Ask the study group to suggest other items that can be added to this list. Explain that most people are tempted by only certain items on this list. We are tempted more by a particular item. Mark that and avoid putting ourselves in a position to be enticed by it.

"Do not be conformed to this world, but be transformed by the renewing of your mind..."
Romans 12:2 NASV

Note

Here are some other Scriptures that attribute untimely physical death to a life of sin: Proverbs 11:19; 12:28; 13:14; 19:16; Exodus 20:12; Ecclesiastes 7:17; 18:13.

Other Scriptures

Ask the study group to turn to these additional examples of the meaning of the phrase *"save your souls."* They can reference these in the margin of their Bible, beside of James 1:15.

When James and John asked if the Lord would command fire down from Heaven and consume a village of Samaritans who would not receive Him, Jesus answered, *"For the Son of man did not come to destroy men's lives, but to save them."* Luke 9:56 NASV. Then in Matthew 20:28, Jesus states, *"The Son of Man did not come to be served, but to serve, and to give His life a ransom for many."*

In Matthew 16:25 Jesus taught His disciples: *"For whoever wishes to save his life shall lose it; but whoever loses his life, for My sake, shall find it."*

The same word *"psyche"* is used for "life" in all these Scriptures.

> *"The fear of the Lord <u>prolongs days</u>, but the <u>years</u> of the wicked will <u>be shortened</u>."*

> Proverbs 10:27 NASV

The context of James chapter one is the same as the above Scripture of wisdom literature. He is saying that believers should lay aside the sinful practices of our life and follow the teachings of God's Word, and become obedient children to the Word of God.

> *"Therefore putting aside all filthiness and all that remains of wickedness, in humility receive the word implanted, which is able to <u>save your souls</u>. But prove yourselves doers of the word, and not merely hearers, who delude themselves."*

> James 1:21-22

James uses the phrase *"save your souls"* here and in chapter 5, verses 19-20 (NASV).

> *"<u>My brethren</u>, if any among you strays from the truth, and one turns him back, let him know that he who turns a sinner from the error of his way will <u>save the soul from death</u>, and will cover a multitude of sins."*

He is still referring to saving a believer's physical life from the deadly results of sin. This phrase is never used in Scripture to refer to being saved from hell. The true meaning is to save a physical life. Jesus Himself used this same phrase when He asked the Pharisees,

> *"Is it lawful on the Sabbath days to do good or to do evil? To <u>save life</u>, or to destroy it?"*

> Luke 6:9 NIV

This is a definition that we had better get straight! James is giving a warning to believers about getting sin out of our life or else! We must not *"delude ourselves"* (v. 22). If we are to have a long, productive Christian life, we cannot be *"hearers only."* For if we choose to disobey God's Word and live a life of sin, the consequences will be a life cut short. Faith alone cannot save a believer's physical life, if he is living a bad testimony. Sin can bring an early end to your earthly days. **Physical** consequences of sin is still the subject when James asks that famous question:

> *"What does it profit, my brethren, if someone says he has faith and does not have works? Can faith save him?"*

> James 2:14 NASV

We can now understand what James is speaking about being saved from. James is warning believers that faith alone cannot save them from the *consequences* of a sinful life, void of good works. Sin does not profit.[25]

> **Faith alone cannot save a Christian's physical life, if he or she is living a bad testimony.**

Since James is talking about prolonging human life by godliness, he is speaking of something that faith along cannot achieve.[26] Just as when Solomon states that the fear of the Lord *"prolongs life"* he is telling us that a prolonged life is the result of our obeying and honoring the Lord. The message that James is telling believers about **temptation**, is that faith (not accompanied by a righteous life) cannot save our physical lives from the deadly consequences of continuing to yield to the enticement to sin.

Yielding to temptation can take away our endurance and crash our hopes of becoming people who are **mature** and **complete**.

Note

This warning in James is important because Christians **are** capable of living disobedient lives. Ask the study group to turn to the following references in their Bible.

- *"For this reason many among you are weak and sick, and a number sleep."* I Corinthians 11:30 (Compare this verse to verses 20-22)

- *"Brethren, if a man is caught in any trespass, you who are spiritual, restore such a one in a spirit of gentleness; each one looking to yourself, **lest you too be tempted**."* Galatians 6:1

It will be helpful to cross-reference these verses in the margin of your Bibles beside of James 2:14.

VICTORY OVER TEMPTATION

A <u>Victory</u> To Win

Back in 1958, a small community in northeastern Pennsylvania built a little red brick building that was to be their police department, their fire department and their city hall. They were proud of that building; it was the result of sacrificial giving and careful planning. When the building was completed, they had a ribbon-cutting ceremony, and more than six thousand of the town's residents were there. It was the biggest event of the year.

Within less than two months, however, they began to notice some ominous cracks on the side of the red brick building.

Sometime later, it was noticed that the windows would not shut all the way. Then it was discovered that the doors wouldn't close correctly. Eventually, the floor shifted and left ugly gaps in the floor covering and corners. The roof began to leak. Within a few more months, it had to be evacuated, to the embarrassment of the builder and the disgust of the taxpayers.

Note

In other Scripture passages, Jesus said:

- *"Take care what you listen to..."* Mark 4:24

- *"Therefore take care how you listen..."* Luke 8:18

- *"And after He called the multitude to Him, He said to them, 'Hear and understand...'"* Matthew 15:10

  The Bible says that it is possible to become dull of hearing.

- *"...we have much to say, and it is hard to explain, since you have become dull of hearing."* Hebrews 5:11

A firm did an analysis shortly thereafter and found that the blasts from a nearby mining area were slowly but effectively destroying the building. **Imperceptibly**, down beneath the foundation, there were small shifts and changes taking place that caused the whole foundation to crack. You couldn't feel it or even see it from the surface, but quietly and down deep there was a weakening. A city official finally had to write across the door of the building, "Condemned. Not fit for public use." Ultimately, the building had to be demolished.[1]

There's an enemy working to destroy all the firmness in our lives, so that, someday we will be unfit for use. The destruction goes unnoticed when you play with temptation until your character is permanently damaged. But there's a way to defeat that enemy. There's a way to win the battle against temptation.

A Strategy To Follow

Victory in times of temptation is dependent upon three responses stated in the Bible.

> **"My dear brothers, take note of this; Everyone should be <u>quick to listen</u>, <u>slow to speak</u> and <u>slow to become angry</u>, for man's anger does not bring about the righteous life that God desires."**
>
> James 1:19-20 NIV

1—Be quick to hear.

The very first step in times of temptation is to "hear" what the Word of God has to say. Notice that we are to be *"quick to hear."* The reason that we must be quick to hear the truth of Scripture is that our thought process in yielding to a temptation (thought, fantasy, desire, choice) often happens in a matter of seconds.[2] We must seek to hear God's wisdom immediately, before we have gone too far into the process and find it too late to resist.

Quickness of hearing becomes possible when we have committed the key Truth to memory. God's wisdom is the most important influence we can have, because it is able to save our life. Notice the way to listen to this life-saving Word is with moral righteousness and a humble heart.

"Therefore, get rid of all moral filth and the evil that is so prevalent and <u>humbly accept the Word planted in you, which can save you</u>."

James 1:21 NIV

Wisdom is derived from the Scriptures, when we take time to *"listen."* James is referring to our listening with undivided attention, without interruption or daydreaming or planning our own response. The first step in victory over temptation is listening to God's moral guidelines with a cleansed and humble heart. Listen to the wisdom of Proverbs.

"Discretion will protect you, and understanding will guard you. Wisdom will save you from the ways of wicked men, from men whose words are perverse, who leave the straight paths to walk in dark ways."

Proverbs 2:11-13 NIV

"Know also that wisdom is sweet to your soul; if you find it, there is a future hope for you, and your hope will not be cut off."

Proverbs 24:14 NIV

The Bible is your map to help you navigate through the rough waters of temptation. Hear what it has to say as your first response.

2—Be…slow to speak

James is telling us not to make a verbal response to the temptation too soon. In times of temptation, it is too easy to allow our emotions to control our words. Proverbs says,

"Where there are many words, transgression is unavoidable, but he who restrains his lips is wise."

Proverbs 10:19 NASV

What are your first words, when faced with temptation? It is easy to begin speaking to yourself right away an effort to rationalize the situation and justify making the wrong choice.

Note

Here are some additional references to turn to as a study group. Remember to reference these in the margin next to James 1:19.

- *"Death and life are in the power of the tongue…"* Proverbs 18:21

- *"He that has knowledge spares his words…"* Proverbs 17:27

- *"An evil man is ensnared by the transgression of his lips, but the righteous will escape from trouble."* Proverbs 12:13

Discussion

Ask the members of the study group if they can think of some good questions to ask ourselves, which will help prevent our giving into a temptation.

Here are several that Charles Stanley suggests:

- *"Is this idea in keeping with God's Word?"*

- *"What are the consequences (both immediate and long term) if I yield to this temptation?"*

- *"What are the consequences to others around me (family and friends)?"*

- *"Am I prepared to pay these consequences— that I will lose far more than I will gain?"*[3]

"Sin is the fulfillment of a legitimate need in an illegitimate way."

Larry Crabb

Morally Unfaithful

The following is an incomplete list of what you have in store after giving in to the temptation of marital infidelity:

- Your mate will experience the anguish of betrayal, shame, rejection, heartache, and loneliness. No amount of repentance will soften the blows.

- Your mate can never again say that you are a model of fidelity. Suspicion will rob her or him of trust.

- Your escapade(s) will introduce to your life and your mate's life the very real probability of sexually transmitted disease.

- The total devastation that your sinful actions will bring to your children is immeasurable. Their growth, innocence, trust and healthy outlook on life will be severely and permanently damaged.

- The heartache you will cause your parents, your family, and your peers is indescribable.

(continued on next page)

There are several areas to direct our speech, which will slow down our decision about the enticement.

✦ Speak To God First

Speak to the Lord in prayer, voicing your request for grace, wisdom and understanding to stand up to temptation and say, **"No!"**

Then voice your commitment to Him to obey His Word: *"Father, I am tempted to make the wrong choice, but I am choosing to do things Your way and rely on You to enable me to live morally, kindly and honestly, as Your ambassador."* (A whole new world has opened to you since you have become a Christian. You represent Christ, therefore, you have a responsibility to be victorious in your battle against temptation.)

✦ Speak To Yourself

We need to talk some things over with ourselves before we make a decision. Charles Stanley in his book, *Walking Wisely*, offers this advice in overcoming the temptation:

> *We all have legitimate needs (love, attention, approval, appreciation, self-esteem, etc.). Temptation will strike in one of these areas that is not being fulfilled. Ask yourself immediately in the face of temptation, "Is there any way—a good way, a right way—of getting this need met in my life?"*[2]

> **Temptation strikes at the area of need that is not being fulfilled. —Charles Stanley**

✦ Speak To The Temptation

When you say **"No!"** to temptation, you are usually talking to some person, so you must say it in such a way that the person who is tempting you will know that you mean business.

Don't say, *"I don't <u>think</u> I should do this."* That response is too weak. The other person will be thinking that you are only partially convinced that the action is wrong. They will then apply more pressure to convince you to give in.

You should say, *"I am not willing to do this,"* or *"I am not choosing to do this."* (Then state your biblical reason for the decision). By stating your decision in this manner, the other person realizes that you have thought it through and reached a firm conclusion. They will then be less likely to offer more enticement.

By praying first, you know that you have God's strength to back you up. He will always enable you to do what is moral and just.

✦ Speak With Your Actions

A good illustration as to how this can be done is given by Donald Barnhouse, in his commentary on *Romans*, volume 4.

A man I knew through my ministry was going with a girl, who some of us thought, was not at all worthy of him. We breathed a sigh of relief when he went away into the army for several years (this was during the war). The girl drifted around with other fellows, and the young man met a worthy girl in a distant city. He fell in love with her and married her. When the war was over and he had returned to his home with his bride, the first girl drove by the house one evening and dropped in to see her old flame and meet his wife. But the wife was not there. The first girl made no attempt to hide her affection and moved in such a way that the young man realized that he had but to reach out his hand and she was his. He told me about it afterwards. There was within him all that goes with male desire. But there was also something much more within him, and he began to talk about what a wonderful girl he had married. He showed the pictures of his wife to the first girl and praised his wife to the skies, acting as though he did not understand her obvious advances. It was not long before she left, saying as she went, "Yes, she must be quite a girl if she can keep you from reaching out to me."*

The young man was never more joyful in his life. He said that in that moment all of the love between him and his wife was

(continued from previous page)

- The embarrassment of facing other Christians, who once appreciated you, respected you, and trusted you, will be overwhelming.

- If you are engaged in the Lord's work, you will suffer immediate loss of your job and the support of those with whom you worked. The dark shadow will accompany you everywhere…and forever. Forgiveness won't erase it.

- Your fall will give others license to do the same.

- The inner peace you enjoyed will be gone.

- You will never be able to erase the fall from your (or others') mind. This will remain indelibly etched on your life's record, regardless of your later return to your senses.

- The name of Jesus Christ, whom you once honored, will be tarnished, giving the enemies of the faith further reason to sneer and jeer.

Charles Swindoll,
The Finishing Touch

Memory Verse

James 1:19

Other Scripture

Here are some additional verses from the New Living Translation about anger.

- "Those who control their anger have great understanding; those with a hasty temper will make mistakes." Proverbs 14:29

- "It is better to be patient than powerful; it is better to have self-control than to conquer a city." Proverbs 16:32

- "People with good sense restrain their anger, they earn esteem by overlooking wrongs." Proverbs 19:11

- "Don't be quick tempered, for anger is the friend of fools." Ecclesiastes 7:9

greater and more wonderful than ever; he could think of his wife in a clean, noble way.

Some people might scoff at him, deriding him for "sacrificing" his pleasure, but the truth is that the turning of his heart and mind and soul and body, to the love of his true wife was the living sacrifice which praised her and made him all the more noble because of it. In this sense he presented his body as a living sacrifice to his Lord.[5]

Identify the temptation that gives you the most trouble and practice speaking with your actions. There's a victory to win!

3—Be...slow to anger.

The most common reaction to difficult times is yielding to the temptation to become angry at those who have treated us unfairly. It's easy to blame others and blame God for our circumstances. James explains:

> **"Be...slow to anger; for the anger of man does not achieve the righteousness of God."**
>
> James 1:19-20 NIV

Anger blocks the development of practical righteousness that God wants to produce in our character.

There *are* times when anger is appropriate. Psalm 97:10 says that he who loves the Lord must hate evil. Ephesians 4:26 tells us to become angry and yet do not sin. So, anger at the appropriate object is not a sin in itself. Therefore our response is not to resolve to *never* be angry, but rather to be "...**slow** to anger."

The idea is that we should control our "hair-trigger" temper—one that is easily set off without control.[6] Godly wisdom, about our response to others, looks like this:

> **"But the wisdom that comes from Heaven is first of all pure; then <u>peace-loving</u>, <u>considerate</u>, <u>submissive</u>, full of <u>mercy</u> and good fruit, impartial and sincere. Peace makers who sow in peace raise a harvest of righteousness."**
>
> James 3:17-18 NIV

Controlling anger also has a great deal to do with who we talk to first, in times of temptation. Some will say that we should express all that is in our heart, and that if we repress (stuff) our feelings, we could cause psychological damage. Therefore we should freely express all our feelings to the other person.

Larry Crabb correctly explains that *the opposite of repressing our feelings is acknowledging them (not **expressing** them).*[5] We should acknowledge to our selves exactly how angry we are, then talk about these feelings with our Lord. As we talk over our hurt with Christ, we must humble ourselves and ask Him to have His peace to rule in our heart in the place of our controlling anger. The reason for this request is because He has called us to live in peace. Ask Him to give us the grace to express our feelings to the other person in His words instead of our own expression of anger. Ask Him for the ability to speak to those, who have offended us, only in a way that will build them up (edify).

Resisting the temptation to improperly express anger, as we walk through the sensitive territory of conflicts in relationships, will enable the other person to respond with an openness to also speak the truth in love. God uses relationships to bring about healing to our souls.

If we align ourselves with these three responses (1) quick to hear, (2) slow to speak, and (3) slow to anger, we can have **Victory Over Temptation**. If we become a doer of God's Word, we will not wear out our lives as defeated believers, who fail in battle to resist temptation.

Tony Evans compares the front end alignment of an automobile to our own spiritual alignment to the principles of God's Word.

> **Most of us have experienced** our cars being out of alignment, when we hit a large pot hole in the road. When your car is not aligned, you don't always feel it, but one of the sure ways to know that it needs alignment is to have your front tires checked. When a car has lost its alignment, there is an uneven wearing away of the front tires.
>
> But, people who are not aware of this, spend time changing tires.
>
> They do not know that the extra wear on the front tires is not due to a tire problem, but rather an alignment problem that is causing their tires to wear out.[7]

"And let the peace that comes from Christ rule in your hearts. For as members of one body you are all called to live in peace. And always be thankful. Let the words of Christ, in all their richness, live in your hearts and make you wise. Use His words to teach and counsel each other... And whatever you do or say, let it be as a representative of the Lord Jesus, all the while giving thanks through Him to God the Father."

Colossians 3:15-17 NIV

Memory Verse
Galatians 6:7

Because of being out of alignment with the biblical responses to temptation, we look at our lives and we see the tread *wearing out* fast. We are seeing more defeat than victory. Every month or so we feel like we need a new set of spiritual tires, when in reality, what we need is spiritual alignment with God's plan for a Biblical response.

If we continue to be out of alignment, we're going to *wear out* the new tires just like we wore out the old ones. There **must** be an alignment where we place ourselves under the authority of God. You might not feel different at first, but you will see the effects of the tread of your life.[8]

Here's The Truth About Consequences
(So you won't be deceived)

Whatever decisions we make in life—good or bad—enduring trials or resisting temptation, we will most definitely experience the consequences of our choices. The Bible teaches that our consequences will be that *same kind* as the decision we have made. In other words, bad choices produce bad consequences and good choices produce good consequences. This future-changing truth is known as the principle of sowing and reaping. The Scriptures state it this way:

> *"Do not be deceived, God is not mocked; for whatever a man sows, this he will also reap. For the one who sows to the flesh shall from the flesh reap corruption, but the one who sows to the Spirit shall from the Spirit reap eternal life."*
>
> Galatians 6:7 NASV

> *"Knowing that whatever good thing each one does, this he will receive back from the Lord..."*
>
> Ephesians 6:8 NASV

> *"...they that plow iniquity, and sow wickedness, reap the same."*
>
> Job 4:8 KJV

John W. Lawrence in *The Seven Laws Of The Harvest*, explains:

Since everything reproduces after its kind, we do not sow discord and reap unity; we do not sow sin and reap sanctification; we do not sow hypocrisy and reap holiness of life. He who sows to the flesh will reap just what the flesh can produce. But he that sows to the Spirit will reap what the Spirit can produce.[9]

Many of the situations that we struggle with are explained by the principle of sowing and reaping. What we sow we will reap. Those who are not aware of this Biblical principle would describe these events in life by saying, *"Whatever goes around comes around"* or *"Every kick has a kickback."* However it is phrased, the principle holds true.

We do not actually reap the same thing that we sow, but rather, we reap the same <u>kind</u> as we sow. Just as we plant cotton in our field and expect to receive cotton when harvest time comes around; or we plant wheat in the winter and expect to reap wheat in May, so also when we cheat someone, someday someone will cheat us, or if we lie to someone, someone will someday lie to us. This is why Jesus spoke these words, which we have come to think of as the golden rule.

> **"Therefore, however you want people to treat you, so treat them, for this is the Law and the Prophets."**
>
> Matthew 7:12 NASV

Jesus is saying that, if we treat other people well, we will be treated well by other people. Bill Hybles explains how this works in a conversation that he had, while waiting for a plane to arrive.

One day I met a man in an international airport... He happened to be spitting mad at God for allowing what he thought was an inordinate amount of pain to enter his life. Since I had plenty of time I said, "Why don't you tell me your life story?" He was glad to oblige me by unloading his self-pitying saga. What he hadn't counted on was my listening as closely as I did.

When he finished complaining and indicting God for everything that had gone wrong in his life, I said, "Wow, that's quite a story, but could I ask you a couple of questions? You said your former wife turned into a horrible, evil person. I wonder what

Illustration

Temptation to sow the wrong kind of seeds is like a rattlesnake. LeRoy Eims, makes the following comparison in *Be The Leader You Were Meant To Be*. Rattlesnakes are fairly common where I live. I encounter one almost every summer. It's a frightening experience to see one coiled, looking at you, ready to strike. He's lightening quick and accurate. I have a simple two-point program for handling rattlesnakes; shun and avoid. It's as simple as that. You don't need much insight to figure out what to do with something as dangerous as a diamondback rattler. You don't mess around.[1]

your relationship with her was like before she turned evil. How did you treat her? Were you good to her? Were you faithful to her? Or did you, perhaps, do some stupid things that might have added a little bit to the demise of your marriage?" He admitted that he had done a few stupid things.

Then I said, "And about your tens of thousands of dollars of debt and your tax problems with the government—a simple question here. Did you ever let your spending get a little out of hand? Did you ever spend more than you earned? Did you ever buy anything foolishly or impulsively?" He admitted that he had.

Then I said, "Now you're frustrated because no one will give you a job. Just a question. Were you a model employee? If I called your last three employers, would they be in a stew over losing an employee as great as you?" Well, he had been fired from his last job because he had lost his temper a few times and told his boss where to go—eternally.

Finally I admitted that I am a pastor and told him that I didn't believe God had singled him out for special suffering. "I don't think it's fair to blame Him for any of the problems you're blaming Him for. The Bible says, 'If you sow folly, you will reap heartbreak.' It seems to me that you've sown plenty of folly, and now you're getting a predictable return. My counsel to you is to enroll in the school of wisdom today."[10]

Hybles went on to comment:

I would like to think that *when he reached his destination at the end of that long day, he looked in the mirror in his hotel room and said, "You've gone far enough down a foolish path. You've damaged enough relationships, squandered enough time and energy, wasted enough money, said enough stupid words, shed enough unnecessary tears. You've proven you don't know how to make life work. You've revealed the folly of your ways. It's white-flag surrender time. It's seek-the-wisdom-of-God time.*[11]

Foolishness is focusing on our own self-interests

Wisdom is to stop sowing the wrong things in our life and in the lives of those around us and begin sowing the right things. It might take a while before we see a real significant change in our circumstances, and character, but eventually we will start reaping a different kind of consequences.

Concerning the power to make this change our pattern of living, Andy Stanley says:

> **Like a good parent**, God consistently works to shape your character. And as you know all too well, He is relentless. He loves you too much to let up or to give up... But while God is faithfully working to produce character in you, oddly enough, much of your progress depends on your willingness to cooperate... Imagine the potential if you worked <u>with</u> Him in your life rather than worked <u>around</u> Him. When the two of you are in **alignment**, it unleashes a whole new dimension of God's power in your life.[12]

> ### Imagine the potential if you worked with Him in your life rather than worked around Him.   —Andy Stanley

When we see the big picture...

When we consider God's reason (purpose) for what He is telling us to do, this starts an amazing force into action within our mind. If we will listen with a heart that is open to God's way of thinking, the results of hearing His mind on the subject will perform an awesome transforming effect in our whole being—emotions, intellect, and will.

Our actions come as a result of how we think. Richard Seymour, in his book *All About Repentance*, explains:

> **Let's say that I am a TV-sports-person**, who always stays up to watch the playoffs. As usual, I am excited about the games that will be on tonight, although they will keep me up pretty late. However, I notice on the calendar that tomorrow morning I am scheduled to get up at 4:00 a.m. to go deep-sea fishing with some friends, and I'm driving. This information that I have received from the calendar has caused me to re-think my plans about staying up late to see the play-offs. With this knowledge now in place, my mind is renewed, and I conclude

Note

At other times in the Bible, we see the principle of sowing and reaping played out in people's lives:

- They hanged Haman on the gallows, which he had prepared for Mordecai. Esther 7:10

- Jacob tricked his brother and Father to get the blessing of the firstborn— later Laban tricked Jacob by using the rights of the firstborn. Genesis 29:20-26

- King David killed Uriah; therefore, God said that the sword would never depart from his house. He took Uriah's wife, and the Lord said that his wives would be taken before his eyes. II Samuel 12:9-12

- Paul was responsible for Stephen's being stoned to death. Acts 7:58 Later, Paul was stoned and left for dead himself. Acts 14:19

Note

Ask the members of the study group to underline the word or phrase in this illustration that indicates the involvement of the emotions, intellect, and will.

- **Emotion**: *"I am excited about the game that will be on tonight."*

- **Intellect**: *"I conclude that I should go to bed early."*

- **Will**: *"I turn off the TV and go to bed early."*

Once they have located the proper phrases, ask them to underline that portion in their workbooks.

"Success is to be measured not so much by the position that one has reached in life as by the obstacles, which he has overcome while trying to succeed."

Booker T. Washington

---

that I had better go to bed early in order to get the proper rest, in preparation for the up-coming fishing trip. Therefore, seeing the bigger picture, which includes more than just the playoffs, I turn off the TV and go to bed early—because I'm driving.

By being informed of the big picture, specifically that tomorrow is the big day for the fishing trip, I have been transformed from a late-night-basketball-fan to an early-morning fisherman.

My previous plans were all about staying up late because of my narrow focus only on tonight's sport's agenda. But my routine was overruled by better judgment which came as a result of my new understanding of the big picture, and I end up doing differently.

Charles Stanley gives another example of how our focus can become fixed on one object and keep us from seeing the big picture. Like the person in this picture, he explains:

> **If I am out in the mountains** *on a photography trip, I have a number of options. I can use a wide-angle lens to try to take in the full panorama of a mountain ridge. Or I can put a longer lens on my camera and focus on one aspect of a mountain—a particular ravine or glacier or outcropping of rock. If I put on an extremely long lens, I may be able to focus on the behavior of a single mountain goat or bear. Once I am looking through a strong telephoto lens, I no longer have a sense of the big picture of the mountain scene. I have zeroed in on only one element, and that element dominates my concentration.*[13]

The same thing often happens when we read the Bible. When we focus only on what God is instructing us to do, we lose all sense of the big picture of His plan. We shut out the explanation of His *purpose* and the consequences of our obedience or disobedience.

For example, Paul says that we are to:

"...be transformed by the renewing of your mind..."

Romans 12:2 NASV

This means that the process of our being transformed will be accomplished when we take into our thinking the knowledge about God's *purposes* behind the instruction He gives.

While we tend to focus our attention on the *activity* that God wants us to perform, we often miss out on *understanding* the *reason* and or the *consequences* attached to that task. But when God supplies the reason or the outcome of His instruction, that causes our understanding to be renewed. It opens up a whole new way of thinking so that we can now see why our cooperation with His program is best.

Now when we read in Galatians 6:7 NASV that, *"...whatever a man sows, this he will also reap,"* our understanding about the consequences of sowing and reaping is established. We see that God has built into His principle a result that makes it unwise to sow selfish behavior. The foolishness of our present self-centered style of relating becomes very evident. By understanding the principle of sowing and reaping more fully, our cooperation with His plan becomes an easier step.

God's principle of the harvest has been used in the transformation of our emotions, intellect and will. That change began at the level of our understanding, when we comprehended more of the big picture.

More about the big picture...

At one time we were impatient-doubters who lost heart that God's promises would come through. We were focusing on what we believed to be a reasonable time for the reaping of His promised blessings. But then we learn from the same chapter that harvest does not come immediately after planting.

"And let us not lose heart in doing good, for in due season we shall reap..."

Galatians 6:9 NASV

Illustration

When people have been living a sinful life for a long time, the harvest of consequences (the time of harvest) could be upon them at any moment.

In the early morning of December 28, 1908, an earthquake struck, and 84,000 human beings died. Only a few hours before that devastating earthquake, which laid the beautiful city of Messina and the surrounding districts in ruins, the unspeakable wicked and irreligious condition of some of the inhabitants was expressed in a series of resolutions which were passed against all religious principles. The Christmas edition of their newspaper, *'Il Telefono* (published in Messina), printed an article **daring the Almighty to make Himself known by sending an earthquake, and in three days, the earthquake came!**[16]

Other Scripture

We see from Genesis 8:22 that there is a *"seed time"* and there is a *"harvest time."* We are promised in Proverbs 11:18 that the reward for *"sowing righteousness"* is sure.

In I Corinthians 15:58, we are encouraged that we should be *"steadfast, immovable, always abounding in the work of the Lord, knowing that your toil is not in vain in the Lord."*

This great information is encouraging as we learn that God has a plan based on reasonable and easy–to–understand principles.

"While the earth abides, there is seed time and harvest time...these shall not cease."

Genesis 8:22 NASV

"...He who sows righteousness gets a sure reward."

Proverbs 11:18 NASV

Now instead of being doubters who lose heart, we become believers, who refuse to become weary in well doing, because we reason that God will come through at the proper time. The fact that it is delayed to *another season* does not mean that the promise is false. Our perception of the truth that *it takes a while for the crop to mature* and for harvest time to roll around is the foundation for our attitude of patient expectation, and our action of continually doing good.

How does this work if... we are sowing bad things?

If we think that, since God has not sent any bad consequences our way, so far, for the sinful sowing that we've been into, it looks like we'll get away without having to suffer any ill effects. In our ignorance, we are operating under the principle that:

"Because the sentence against an evil deed is not executed quickly, therefore the hearts of the sons of men among them are given fully to do evil."

Ecclesiastes 8:11 NASV

While we were once people who thought, *"Whew, we got by with it,"* now, after reading that the consequences are sure to come in harvest time, there is a new understanding that, *"We've gone far enough down this foolish path."* We are no longer confident, risk-taking, ignorant sinners, who think that we are getting away with sin. We have been transformed into well informed, repentant followers, who see clearly how foolish it is to defy God's principles.

But some think they can "handle" any consequences that may occur.

These people think like this:

"What's a little slap on the hand, compared to all the fun, fame, wealth, or control we will experience? It couldn't be that bad."

Therefore those, who are uninformed, will reason that it is *"worth the risk"* to have a little fun. They do not realize that the harvest is greater than the sowing.

"He who sows iniquity shall reap calamity..."

Proverbs 22:8 NASV

"They have sown to wind, and they will reap the whirlwind."

Hosea 8:7 NASV

At harvest time, we gather far more than we planted months before. We reap more than we sow. We should comprehend that the consequences are far, far more than a "slap on the hand."

Now that we know by the Word of God that the consequences of sowing iniquity are earth-shaking, and having taken this fact into our thinking, we can become transformed from over-confident braggers, who think, **"It couldn't be that bad,"** to sober-minded realists, who are fully convinced that God is powerful enough to handle the "tough guys." So, we wave the white flag and *realign* ourselves with His principles of the harvest.

What we see as important will determine how we choose to sow.

You know what it's like to hear the alarm clock go off early on a cold winter morning— and the thinking process that begins to develop as you contemplate leaving the comfort of the warm covers? It seems only reasonable that the state of sleepiness that you have gotten adjusted to during the night and your current comfortable condition should be the way to spend the entire day. You're all covered up and you don't want any interruption. It is difficult to leave that warm place and get up and put your feet on the cold floor to begin getting ready to go to work.

Tony Evans explains that getting up has to be a decision of the will:

Note

In Proverbs 22:8, the term *"calamity"* refers to *"sorrow, grief, suffering, and anxiety."* Therefore, we see that sowing iniquity brings absolutely devastating consequences.

The word *"whirlwind"* in Hosea 8:7 is speaking of a *"violent, destructive tornado."* This refers to a harvest of breath-taking destruction.[14]

In the New Living Translation of Proverbs 1:25-27, wisdom says, *"You ignored my advice and rejected the correction I offered. So I will laugh when you are in trouble! I will mock you when **disaster overtakes you**—when **calamity overcomes you** like a storm, when you are **engulfed by trouble**, and when **anguish and distress overwhelm you**."*

Illustration

A man was traveling in a foreign city and was alone on a street that had an X-rated theater. No one was there who knew him. Silently he stood in front of the marquee and read the words and looked at a few of the pictures, and he was tempted to go in. As he backed away toward the curb, he remembered, *"I would be true for there are those who trust me. I would be true for there are those who care."* The old hymn that they sang in the church back home came to his rescue. He turned and went on.[1]

Loyalty to those who trust us and care about the choices we make can prompt us to choose how we sow.

You begin to reason that, if you don't get up from that warm, comfortable bed, you won't get to work. You'll lose your job. You won't make any money. You'll be broke and lose your house. You might not feel like getting up. You might not want to get up, but the objective reason for getting up is better than the reason for staying there!

To stay in bed feels good for the moment, but the price tag for that choice is the loss of things that make life possible.

What causes you to get up? The reason for getting up is greater than the comfort of staying in.[15]

> **What causes you to get up? The <u>reason</u> for getting up is <u>greater</u> than the <u>comfort</u> of staying in. —Tony Evans**

The renewing of our thinking process to include God's truth about the harvest and how it works will become the basis for our decisions about our behavior (sowing). This new insight about the effects of our self-centered way of relating can result in a transformed mind, which chooses to:

"...do good to all men, especially to those who are of the household of the faith."

Galatians 6:10 NASV

If we allow Him, the **Holy Spirit** will use the Scriptures to pull back the curtains of our understanding.[17] If we ask, He will renew our mind about this principle, so that our sowing will not stay just like it is at the present and our consequences will not go on as usual.

Remember how the disciples' dedication grew more and more as they continued to follow Christ?

As the disciples first began the process of transformation by renewing their understanding about Jesus Christ, *"they left their nets...boat, and father and followed Him"* (Matthew 4:18-22). Then, as they comprehended more fully who He is, their commitment grew deeper, and they *"left everything and followed Him"* (Luke 5:1-11).

Later, after seeing His great power, as He fed the five thousand and walked on the Sea of Galilee, they were willing to follow in a much deeper sense—even willing to suffer through, *"taking up their cross and following Him"* (Matthew 16:13-28). This is the cost of greater dedication.

As we walk with Jesus Christ, in loyalty to Him and His Word, we are gradually transformed. It's a *JOURNEY* of continuing maturity and increasing commitment to represent the Lord Jesus Christ in our performance on the stage of life. That's when our personal dedication will really show up. It will be your time to let others see what a difference the Lord has made in your life.

You can experience victory through trials and over temptation. Every day of your life, there's a strategy to follow, and there's a victory to win.

As we follow Christ, we will become effective in telling others that Christ has reconciled the world to Himself, and that He is not counting men's sins against them.

We can tell the good news that anyone can have eternal life **by faith in Jesus Christ**.

Note

Return to page 13 and 14 and review how the commitment of the disciples became stronger as they learned more about our Lord Jesus Christ. Turn to each of the Scripture references given in the three different occasions when the disciples grew in their knowledge of Jesus and in their dedication to Him.

Ask the study group to discuss how they might encourage one another to continually allow God's principles to make them more and more like Christ.

"Do not fear, from now on, you will be catching men."
Luke 5:10

JOURNEY

Now we are at a new place in our *JOURNEY*. We see other people, who are just getting started in their Christian life. Some of them think they don't have much of an opportunity to be a part of the act. As newcomers to the Christian community, they see very little demand for their song and dance. Seeing that you and others seemed to have it all together, they assumed that there is no part for an amateur at the moment. So they're just waiting in the wings for a break.

There are other believers out there, just waiting to be discovered.

Well, what do you think? Since God has already sent a few earthquakes and April showers into our life to transform us and make us a lot more like Him, why not help them get their act together? Before you know it, they'll be taking a more dedicated role in the drama of life.

But we don't want to let the curtain drop here. There are other believers out there, just waiting to be discovered. "We ain't seen nothin' yet."*

* This account of the life of Al Jolson came from a Foster Grant advertisement published in *Modern Plastics* magazine, April, 1969.

GET YOUR BONUS STUDENT QUIZZES

Download your free bonus student quizzes today to complement your *JOURNEY* Leader's Guide. These quizzes will guide your students into learning the content of this Bible study material so they can have their character transformed by God through the study of His Word.

Once you have downloaded the PDF, **you can print out and distribute as many copies of these student quizzes as needed**.

Download your FREE PDF quizzes today at:

www.MaxMillsOnline.com/bonusquizzes

END NOTES

Introduction

1. Adapted from Ginger McFarland, Wheaton Illinois, from the July 19, 1999 issue of *Time*, published in *The Pastor's Story File*, (Platteville, CO: Saratoga Press).

2. Source Unknown.

3. Larry Crabb, *Connecting*, (Word Publishing 1997), p.71.

4. Bruce Wilkinson, *Seven Laws of the Learner*, (Walk Through the Bible Ministries, Inc.) p.14.

5. Dan Allender, (Class notes, Grace Theological Seminary, Winona Lake, IN).

6. Ibid.

Chapter 1

1. This account of the life of Al Jolson came from a Foster Grant advertisement published in *Modern Plastics* magazine, April, 1969.

2. Zane C. Hodges, *The Hungry Inherit*. (Dallas, Texas: Redencion Viva, 1997), p.33.

3. Ibid, p.32.

4. Ibid, p.35.

5. Ibid.

6. David Sylvester, editor, *Great Stories*, (San Antonio, Texas:), Vol. 5 / Issue 20, October-December, 1998, p.14.

7. Max Anders, (A concept that was taught in seminary class at Grace Theological Seminary, winter session of 1985).

8. Raymond McHenry, editor, *In Other Words*, (Beaumont, Texas:), Spring, 1999, p.19.

9. Campus Life, January 1996, p.63.

10. In Other Words, Spring, 1999.

11. Source Unknown

12. Thomas Cahill, *Life*, December, 1999, p.68, (This was printed in Parables, etc.) Date unknown.

13. Tony Evans, (Statement from a message given on Ephesians).

14. John Ortberg, *The Life You've Always Wanted*. (Grand Rapids, Michigan: Zondervan, 1997) p.19.

15. Walter Bauer's *A Greek-English Lexiacon of the New Testament and Other Early Christian Literature*. (Chicago and London: The University Of Chicago Press, 1979), p.863.

16. *In Other Words*, (No other information is available.)

17. *In Other Words*, Spring, 1999, p.4.

18. Ibid.

19. Chester A. McCalley, *Window On The Word*, a publication of *Word Of Truth*, Kansas City, Missouri, (date not available).

20. Walter Bauer, *A Greek-English Lexicon of the New Testament and Other Early Christian Literature*. (Chicago and London: The University of Chicago Press, 1979), p.511.

21. John Ortberg, *The Life You've Always Wanted*. p.23.

22. Tony Evans, a message given on Romans 12:1-2.

23. Ibid.

24. Source Unknown.

25. *In Other Words*. Vol. 13, Issue 3, Fall, 2003, p.7.

26. Steve Covey, *First Things First*, 1994, p.88, published in *In Other Words*, Spring, 1999.

27. Ibid.

28. Craig Brian Larson, *Illustrations for Preaching and Teaching*. (Grand Rapids, Michigan: Baker Books, 1993), p.43.

29. Ibid, p.186.

30. Ibid.

31. Ibid. p.21.

32. Ibid.

33. Ibid. p.114.

34. *In Other Words*. Fall 2003, p.10.

35. Chester McCalley, "The Grace of Growing Older," *Window On The Word*, a bi-monthly publication of *Word of Truth*, Kansas City, Missouri.

36. Frank B. Minirth, *Christian Psychiatry*, p.182.

37. This information came from one of my faithful teachers. However, I cannot locate the source.

38. Tony Evans, (adapted from a message given on John 15).

Chapter 2

1. Walter Bauer, *A Greek-English Lexicon of the New Testament and Other Early Christian Literature*. (Chicago and London: The University of Chicago Press, 1979), p.485.

2. Walter Bauer, p.503-504.

3. "To Illustrate," *Leadership*. A Magazine published by *Christianity Today*. (no date located).

4. Zane C. Hodges, *The Gospel Under Siege*. (Dallas, Texas: Redencion Viva, 1992), p.46.

5. Walter A Elwell, *Evangelical Dictionary Of Theology*. (Grand Rapids, Michigan: Baker Book House, 1984), p.2.

6. Robert N. Wilkin, *Confident In Christ*. (Irving, Texas: Grace Evangelical Society, 1999), p.106.

7. Source unknown. (This came from a teacher, but I cannot remember which one.)

8. Walter A. Elwell, *Evangelical Dictionary Of Theology*, p.414. Walter Bauer, *Greek-English Lexicon*, p.438-439.

9. Raymond McHenry, *In Other Words*.

10. James Aggrey, *Journal of Religious Speaking*. (printed in *The Pastor's Story File*, Oct. 1985).

11. Zane Hodges, *The Gospel Under Siege*, p.46

12. Ibid, p.70.

13. Tony Evans, (message given on John 15).

14. *National Geographic*. Included by Craig B. Larson in Illustrations for Preaching and Teaching. (Grand Rapids, Michigan: Baker Books, 1993), p. 236.

15. Michael Hogan, editor, *Pastor's Story File*. (Platteville, CO: Saratoga Press)

16. Larry Crabb, (lecture given in seminary class at Grace Theological Seminary, Winona Lake, IN).

17. Craig B. Larson, *Illustrations for Preaching and Teaching*, p.45.

18. Andy Stanley, (sermon on Fellowship).

19. Zane C. Hodges, *Absolutely Free*. (Grand Rapids, Michigan: Zondervan Publishing House,1989), p.131.

20. Hodges, p.134.

21. Walter Bauer, p.859.

22. Hodges, p.174.

23. Craig B. Larson, p. 146.

24. *The Farm Journal*, printed in *Parables*, etc., edited by Michael Hodgin, (Platteville, CO: Saratoga Press.)

Chapter 3

1. Tony Evans, (message about fellowship).

2. Zane C. Hodges, *The Epistles of John*. (Irving, Texas: Grace Evangelical Society, 1999), p.57.

3. Zane C. Hodges, The Epistles of John. P.60.

4. Tony Evans, (message).

5. Roger Edwards, *How Do You Say, "I'm Sorry?"*. An article printed in *The Barnabas Letter* (Charlotte, NC) issue and date not available.

6. Tony Evans, (message about fellowship).

7. Roger Edwards, *How Do You Say, "I'm Sorry?"*

8. Ibid.

9. Walter Bauer, *A Greek-English Lexicon Of The New Testament and Other Early Christian Literature.* (Chicago and London: The University Of Chicago Press, 1979), p.568.

10. John Ortberg, *The Life You've Always Wanted.* (Grand Rapids, Michigan: Zondervan, 1997), p.124.

11. *Pastor's Weekly Briefing*, Focus on the Family, 2/11/00 p.2, printed in *In Other Words*, edited by Raymond McHenry, (no other information).

12. Marshall Shelley, editor, *Leadership Magazine.* Published by *Christianity Today.* (other information unknown).

13. Bob Richards, (Olympic Gold Metal winner) used this story in a speech, 1950's.

14. John Ortberg, *The Life You've Always Wanted*, p.119-120.

15. Ortberg, p.120-121.

16. Zane Hodges, *The Epistles of John.* P. 65.

17. Walter Bauer, *Greek-English Lexicon*, p.17-18.

18. Andy Stanley, *Like A Rock*, (Nashville, TN: Thomas Nelson Publishers, 1997).

19. Ibid.

20. Marginal note in the *New American Standard Bible.* Reference Edition, (Nashville, Tennessee: Holman Bible Publishers, 1977).

21. Craig B. Larson, *Illustrations for Preaching and Teaching.* (Grand Rapids, Michigan: Baker Book House, 1993), p.123.

22. Craig B. Larson, *Illustrations for Preaching and Teaching*, p.192.

23. Larry Crabb, *The Pressure's Off.* (Colorado Springs, Colorado: WaterBrook Press, 2002), p.18.

24. Larry Crabb, *The Pressure's Off*, p.8.

25. Walter Bauer, *Greek-English Lexicon*, p.618.

26. Zane Hodges, *The Epistles of John*, p.69-70.

27. Craig B. Larson, p.242.

28. Leadership, magazine (date unknown).

29. Dave Roever, (printed in a fund-raising letter).

30. Chester McCalley, *Window On The Word.* A publication of *Word Of Truth*, (Kansas City, MO).

Chapter 4

1. Developed from several sources, including Andy Stanley and Tony Evans.

2. Unknown.

3. Michael Hodgin, editor, *The Pastor's Story File.* (Platteville, CO: Saratoga Press), March, 2001.

4. Walter Bauer, *A Greek-English Lexicon Of The New Testament and Other Early Christian Literature.* (Chicago and London: The University Of Chicago Press, 1979), p.511.

5. Bruce Bugbee, *What You Do Best.* (Grand Rapids, Michigan: Zondervan Publishing House, 1995) p.83-84.

6. Andy Stanley, *Like A Rock,* (Nashville, TN: Thomas Nelson Publishers, 1997), p.137.

7. Stephen R. Covey, *The Seven Habits of Highly Effective People* (New York: Simon and Schuster, 1989), p.30-31. Covey's experience is also recorded in Joseph Dillow's book, *The Reign of the Servant Kings* (Hayesville, NC: Schoettle Publishing Co., 1993), p.25-26.

8. John Ortberg, *The Life You've Always Wanted* (Grand Rapids, Michigan: Zondervan 1997), p.51.

9. Andy Stanley, (presented in a message on character).

10. Larry Crabb, (class notes from Grace Theological Seminary).

11. T. D. Griffith, *The Four Faces of Freedom* (Rapid City, South Dakota: Mount Rushmore National Memorial Society, 1992), p.31.

12. Larry Crabb, (Class lecture at Grace Theological Seminary, Winona Lake, Indiana).

13. Bruce Bugbee, *What You Do Best,* Grand Rapids, Michigan: Zondervan Publishing House, 1995), p.47-48.

14. Ibid, p.48.

15. *The Biblical Evangelist,* March 1989. The Real Elvis Presley.

16. *The Christian Reader,* January / February, 1997, p.101.

17. Craig B. Larson, *Illustrations for Preaching and Teaching,* (Grand Rapids, Michigan: Baker Books, 1993), p.223.

* Marginal quotes are from Criswell Freeman, editor, *The Wisdom of Southern Football,* (Nashville, Tennessee: Walnut Grove Press, 1995).

Chapter 5

* Marginal quotes are from Criswell Freeman, *The Wisdom of Southern Football,* (Nashville, TN: Walnut Grove Press, 1995).

2. Billy Graham, (Message).

3. Ibid.

4. Craig B. Larson, *Illustrations for Preaching and Teaching,* (Grand Rapids, Michigan: Baker Books, 1993), p. 102.

5. Raymond McHenry, *In Other Words,* (Beaumont, Texas).

6. C. S. Lewis, Mere Christianity, p. 164. This story was given in Howard Hendricks' book *Standing Together,* and *Stories For A Man's Heart,* p.97.

7. Michael Hodgin, *The Pastor's Story File,* (Platteville, CO: Saratoga Press), date unknown.

8. Winston Churchill, (postcard from Fairchild Air Force Base, Spokane, Washington).

9. Craig B. Larson, Illustrations for Preaching and Teaching, p.222.

10. Walter Bauer, *A Greek-English Lexicon Of The New Testament and Other Early Christian Literature,* (Chicago and London: The University Of Chicago Press, 1979), p.105.

12. Tony Evans, (message on II Peter).

13. Zane C. Hodges, "An Exposition of 2 Peter 1:5-11," an article that appeared in the Journal of the Grace Evangelical Society, Spring, 1998, p.23.

14. Ibid.

15. Walter Bauer, *A Greek–English Lexicon Of The New Testament*, p.163.

16. Zane C. Hodges, "An Exposition of 2 Peter 1:5-11," p.23.

17. Charles R. Swindoll, *Growing Deeper In The Christian Life, The Bible*, (Nashville, TN: Broadman Press, 1986), p.26.

18. Ravi Zacharias, "Being A Man Of The Word" included in the book, *A Life Of Integrity*, edited by Howard Hendricks, (Sisters, Oregon: Multnomah Books, 1997), p.53.

19. Tony Evans, (message).

20. William Arthur Ward, quoted by Edsel Burleson in *The World Evangelist*, (no other information).

21. Charles Stanley, *Walking Wisely*, (Nashville, TN: Thomas Nelson Publishers, 2002), p.114.

22. Ibid. p.122.

23. Chester A. McCalley, *Window On The Word*, a publication of *Word of Truth*, (Kansas City, MO).

24. Ibid.

25. Ibid.

26. Zane C. Hodges, p.24.

27. Ibid.

28. Ibid.

29. Zane C. Hodges, The Epistles of John, (Irving, Texas: Grace Evangelical Society, 1999), p.160.

30. Tony Evans, (message).

31. This entire explanation is given by Zane C. Hodges in *The Epistles of John*, p.161.

32. Zane C. Hodges, p.183.

33. Ibid, p.185.

34. Ibid, p.81.

35. Ibid, p.75.

36. Raymond McHenry, *In Other Words*, (Beaumont, Texas).

37. Walter Bauer, *A Greek-English Lexicon Of The New Testament*, p.667.

38. Walter Bauer, p.104.

39. Hodge, "An Exposition Of Second Peter 1:5-9," p.27.

40. Bruce Bugbee, *What You Do Best*, (Grand Rapids, Michigan: Zondervan Publishing House, 1995), p.46.

41. Andy Stanley, *Like A Rock*, (Nashville, TN: Thomas Nelson Publishers, 1997)

42. Marshall Shelley, editor, *Leadership*, a publication of *Christianity Today*, Fall 2000, p.65.

43. Unknown

Chapter 6

1. Stephen R. Covey, *The Seven Habits of Highly Effective People*, *Restoring The Character Ethic* (New York, London, Sydney, Singapore: Free Press, 1989), p.96.

2. Ibid, p.98.

3. Raymond McHenry, In Other Words, (Beaumont, Texas:) Fall 2000, p.3.

4. Although this was not a statement made by Zane C. Hodges, the idea of the human heart being a road of thoughts comes from his book, *The Hungry Inherit*, 3rd Edition (Dallas, Texas: Redencion Viva, 1997), p.67.

5. Joseph C. Dillow, *The Reign Of The Servant Kings*, (Hayesville, NC: Schoettle Plublishing Co., 1992), p.398.

6. Robert N. Wilkin, *Confident In Christ*, (Irving, Texas: Grace Evangelical Society, 1999), p.27.

7. Unknown.

8. Wayne Dehoney, *Illustration Digest*, (No other information available).

9. H. Jackson Brown, Jr., *A Hero In Every Heart*, (Thomas Nelson, 1996), p.104.

10. Raymond McHenry, editor, *In Other Words*, (Beaumont, Texas: Spring, 1999), p.12.

11. James E. White, "Sacred Acts, Baptism," a taped message given at Mecklenburg Community Church, Charlotte, NC.

12. Arthur L. Farstad, "Water Baptism," an article in the *Journal of the Grace Evangelical Society*, (Dallas, Texas:), Vol. 3, No. 1, Spring 1990, p. 9.

13. Walter Bauer, *A Greek-English Lexicon Of The New Testament and Other Early Christian Literature*, (Chicago and London: The University Of Chicago Press, 1979), p.131.

14. Arthur L. Farstad, "Water Baptism," p.7.

15. H. A. Ironside, *Wrongly Dividing the Word of Truth*, p.56, quoted in the article by Arthur Farstad, "Water Baptism," p.9.

Chapter 7

1. Garry Friesen, *Decision Making & the Will of God*, (Portland, Oregon: Multnomah Press, 1980), p.185-187.

2. Bill Hybles, *Who You Are When No One's Looking*, (Downers grove, Illinois: InterVarsity Press, 1987), p. 42.

3. Joseph M. Stowell, *The Dawn's Early Light*, (Chicago, IL: Moody Press, 1990), p.35-36.

4. Marshall Shelley, editor, *Leadership Magazine*, a publication of *Christianity Today International*.

5. Joseph Stowell, *The Dawn's Early Light*, p.37.

6. Joseph Stowell, p.38.

7. Ibid, p.39.

8. John Ortberg, *The Life You've Always Wanted*, (Grand Rapids, Michigan: Zondervan, 1997). p.142.

9. Unknown.

10. Bill Hybles, *Making Life Work*, (Downers Grove, Illinois: InterVarsity Press, 1998), p.68.

11. Tony Evans, given in a message on II and III John.

12. Raymond McHenry, editor, *In Other Words*, (Beaumont, Texas:)

13. Zane C. Hodges, *The Epistle of James*, (Irving, Texas: Grace Evangelical Society, 1994), p.20.

14. Gary Friesen, *Decision Making & the Will of God*, p.195.

15. Ibid, p.197.

16. Ibid.

17. Joseph Stowell, p.40.

18. Ibid.

19. Bill Hybles, *Making Life Work*, p.76.

20. Ibid. p.74.

21. J. Vernon McGee, *Thru The Bible*, (Nashville, TN: Thomas Nelson Publishers, 1983), Vol. 5, p.629.

22. Walter A. Elwell, *Evangelical Dictionary of Theology*, (Grand Rapids, Michigan: Baker Book House, 1984), p. 537.

23. Chester A. McCalley, (a tape series on the book of Proverbs).

24. J. Vernon McGee, *Thru The Bible*, Vol. 3, p.7.

25. Zane C. Hodges, *The Epistle of James*, p.21.

26. Gary Friesen, p.195.

27. Ibid, p.98.

28. Ibid.

29. Bill Hybles, *Making Life Work*, p.195-196.

30. Ibid.

31. Raymond McHenry, *In Other Words*, (Beaumont, Texas:) date and issue is not known.

32. This story was printed on an illustration calendar (February, 20th).

33. Gary Friesen, p.152.

34. Craig Brian Larson, *Illustrations for Preaching and Teaching*, (Grand Rapids, Michigan: Baker Books, 1993), p.176.

35. Marshall Shelley, editor, *Leadership Magazine* (no date or page available).

Chapter 8

1. Unknown.

2. Neva Coyle, *The Pastor's Story File*, (Platteville, CO: Saratoga Press).

3. Tony Evans, (Message on James 1:2)

4. Craig Brian Larson, *Illustrations for Preaching and Teaching*, (Grand Rapids, Michigan: Baker Books, 1993), p.265.

5. Tony Evans, (message about Hebrews Chapter 5). This illustration about "practice" was adapted from that message.

6. Ibid.

7. Ibid.

8. Robert N. Wilkin, *Confident In Christ*, (Irving, Texas: Grace Evangelical Society, 1999), p.146.

9. Unknown.

10. Joseph M. Stowell, *The Dawn's Early Light*, (Chicago, IL: Moody Press, 1990), p.102.

11. Ibid.

12. Chester A McCalley, *Window On The Word*, a publication of *Word of Truth*, Kansas City, MO.

13. Ibid.

14. Raymond McHenry, editor, *In Other Words*, (Beaumont, Texas).

15. Unknown.

16. Chester A. McCalley, *Window On The Word*.

17. Maxie Dunnam, *Jesus Claims—Our Promises*. This illustration was written in *Illustrations for Preaching and Teaching*, edited by Craig Brian Larson, p.21.

18. Bill Donahue and Russ Robinson, *Building A Church Of Small Groups*, (Grand Rapids, Michigan: Zondervan, 2001), p.83-84.

19. Ibid, p.81.

20. James W. Cox, editor, *The Minister's Manual*, (Harper-Collins, 1994), p.63.

21. Tony Evans, (Message on James 1:2)

22. Charles F. Stanley, *Walking Wisely*, (Nashville, TN: Thomas Nelson Publishers, 2002), p.114.

23. Ibid, p.116.

24. Bill Donahue, *Building A Church Of Small Groups*, p.115.

25. Zane C. Hodges, Absolutely Free, (Dallas, Texas: Redencion Viva, 1989), p.124.

26. Ibid, p.125.

27. Charles F. Stanley, Walking Wisely, p. 123.

28. Ibid, p.124.

29. Ibid.

Chapter 9

1. Charles R. Swindoll, *Hand Me Another Brick*, included in his book, *The Tale of the Tardy Oxcart*, (Nashville, TN: Word Publishing, 1998), p.560-561.

2. Charles F. Stanley, *Walking Wisely*, (Nashville, TN: Thomas Nelson Publishers, 2002), p.123.

3. Ibid, p.124.

4. Charles Swindoll, *The Tale of the Tardy Oxcart*, p.565.

5. Larry Crabb, classroom lecture at Grace Theological Seminary, Winona Lake, Indiana.

6.   Zand C. Hodges, *The Epistle of James*, (Irving, Texas: Grace Evangelical Society, 1994)

7.   Tony Evans, (Message on James 4:7-12).

8.   Ibid.

9.   John W. Lawrence, *The Seven Laws Of The Harvest*, (Grand Rapids, Michigan: Kregel Publications, 1975), p.38.

10. Bill Hybels, *Making Life Work*, (Downers Grove, Illinois: Inter Varsity Press, 1998), p.23-24.

11. Ibid.

12. Andy Stanley, *Like A Rock*, (Nashville, TN: Thomas Nelson Publishers, 1997), p.135.

13. Charles F. Stanley, *Walking Wisely*, p.131.

14. John W. Lawrence, *The Seven Laws Of The Harvest*, p.62.

15. Tony Evans, (Message on the book of James).

16. Louis S. Bauman, quoted in the "Sunday School Times." Included by John W. Lawrence in *The Seven Laws Of The Harvest*, p.51.

17. Charles Stanley, p.21.

18. Frank Minirth and Paul Meier, *Happiness Is a Choice*, quoted by Charles Swindoll in *The Tale of the Tardy Oxcart*, p.188.

19. Charles Swindoll, p.188.